Running for the B-Team

Running for the B-Team

One man's obsessive quest
to run a marathon in under 3 hours

Mike Bannister

First Published in Great Britain 2015

by Mike Bannister

Illustrations by Matt Lambert

Rear Cover Photo by Alan Field

This is the year. This is my race. For all the doubters, for all those who have believed in me, for myself, for my sanity, for my children, for my grandchildren*, to be etched in history for ever and never taken away from me, tomorrow morning I'm going to break 3 hours.

**It might be worth mentioning that I don't actually have any grandchildren. In fact, come to think of it, I don't have any children either. But if one day I do, well, I guess it would be a nice touch if this were, in part, for them!*

Forewords

Running for the B-Team is a lovely comical account of a journey to become a sub-3hr marathon runner. This is a story of determination, a never-give-up attitude and meticulous attention to detail (albeit often in the wrong areas)! Mike Bannister's ability to laugh at himself, as well as ridicule his running mates and portray the funny side of an array of running situations, makes this a most amusing and entertaining read.

Mike Gratton

Commonwealth Games Bronze Medallist (1982)

London Marathon Winner (1983)

Owner of 2:09 Events

Mike will tell you that no race begins at the start line. To run your perfect race is all about preparing well. In this book Mike presents his personal story to argue this point. You're left in no doubt that he loves and lives for his running. Less obvious perhaps is how he has persevered in his journey, both to achieve his running goal and to put his story into print. It's worth reading!

Richard Nerurkar

World Cup Marathon Winner (1993)

Olympic Marathon 5th Place (1996)

Contents

Introduction

Despite in no way being an elite athlete, over the past 15 years I have acquired a fair bit of experience of marathon running and the associated inescapable months of preparation that precede the big day. In the pages that follow, I have attempted to take a light-hearted look at the countless wonderful experiences enjoyed... and suffered! These have been shared with a delightful spectrum of people along the way, many of whom I am proud to call my friends. Hindered by a catalogue of minor injuries, I have maintained focus and remained determined to achieve the goal I set myself all those years ago. I have come to realise that to succeed in running is not a case of 'one size fits all' and, consequently, I have continually experimented with new ways to hopefully improve both speed and endurance.

All I wanted to do was complete a marathon in under 3 hours. To put things into perspective, my personal best time for a half marathon is 1 hour 22 minutes and that was in Hastings, one of the hilliest road half marathons in the UK. Having studied various conversion tables to estimate an achievable marathon time, I really ought to be able to knock out a sub-3. In fact, my marathon times to date are as follows:

3:08, 3:15, 3:02, 3:02, 3:28, 3:09, 3:03.

Seven marathons in 15 years might not sound like a lot. However, I have entered and trained for considerably more than actually run. This is quite simply because, on a number of occasions, one injury or another has prevented me from making it to the start line. With no particular pattern of time-out other than: run, get injured, run, get injured, run, get injured, periods of abstinence have ranged from a few days to 18 months.

Throughout my chain of attempts and failures, I have been increasingly subjected to extensive ridicule from supposed mates, who have found great amusement in my seemingly never-ending mission. These 'mates' are predominantly those who have already completed a marathon in '2-something'!

I am not deterred. The repetitive knock-backs and continual testing of my belief that I can do this has made me even more determined.

If I had realised back then what it would take for me to reach this ridiculous and pointless target, perhaps I would have directed my energy elsewhere. But it has by no means been a waste of time. I have kept myself fit and healthy in the process (excepting short term injuries), developed a wonderful social circle and travelled to some fantastic places made possible through an array of running events. My route to sub-3 has consequently taken me on a course that has left me with many treasured memories and I am delighted to share these with you.

On a trip to Ethiopia, I had the privilege of mingling with some incredibly talented runners, including the man widely acknowledged as being the greatest athlete of all time. Without doubt, natural ability must play a significant part in reaching the highest level. Of course, I never had any intention of reaching the highest level. I simply set myself what I thought was a realistic target and, thereafter, have spent an inordinate proportion of my life, for some bizarre reason, trying to get there.

For anyone new to marathon running, hopefully this book provides an insight into what amazing experiences may be waiting for you. Furthermore, I would like to think that sharing my own personal account will in some way help you prepare to reach your own target for the 26.2 miles that lie ahead. Just don't take it too seriously! For those of you still on a mission to improve after numerous attempts, I shall be delighted if you should happen to find an odd tip to help you get around the course just a little bit faster.

So, this is my story, a story about a journey, and I've almost arrived!

Having only ever run marathons in the UK, I now find myself making my final preparations to run one of the fastest courses in the world. The race is now just hours away. This time, I'm going to do it!

Chapter 1

Beetroot Shots and Gel-Flapping-Reduction Strategies

I'm sitting in a cafe on the corner of Pariser Platz with Fiona and Glasses Chris, a couple of hundred metres from the Brandenburg Gate. I periodically raise my head to survey the constant to-ing and fro-ing of tourists and to dip in and out of conversation. This serves no purpose other than to distract me from writing my pre-race plan which, so far, has taken all morning and half the afternoon. Today is Saturday 24th September 2011 and tomorrow is the Big Day.

Fiona and I arrived in Berlin on Thursday evening. Having alighted from our train from the airport, we enjoyed a delightful walk which took us, unexpectedly, past a smattering of friendly ladies of the night. We had inadvertently booked our hotel in the middle of the red light district. We picked up our pace and managed to avoid being propositioned. Our stay on Oranienburger Straβe was to be brief. The group of us running the marathon tomorrow has evolved over a period of several months. All committing to the event at different times has meant that those who came on board later found that flight costs had risen and hotels had filled up to capacity. The consequence of this was that we were to fly out at different times, on different days, from different airports and stay at different hotels. Some of us are also switching hotels, mid-stay, so that at least we shall all be together on the eve of the race.

Glasses Chris* met Fiona and me, mid hotel-switch, at Alexanderplatz station yesterday morning. From there, we traipsed across town to the reception hall of the former

**Glasses Chris's real name is Chris, but he's an optician and he also wears glasses so we tend to call him Glasses Chris.*

Tempelhof Airport, the venue for the marathon expo, where we were to register and collect our running numbers. This should have been a relatively straightforward exercise. Well, it was for Fiona and me. Glasses Chris, however, had made a huge faux-pas. He came to Germany without his race registration document. Unfortunately, the officials were unable to accommodate his error.

To be fair, Glasses Chris could not be held solely accountable for this oversight. In fact, he doesn't actually have an official entry. He's only here because Paul, a mutual friend from the Brighton running scene, decided a month ago that he would give up his entry as there was no way he was going to be fit enough to make it to the start line. He used some lame excuse like needing a knee operation. Paul, alias Goat Boy, used to represent Wales in cross-country races. Evidently, all the bounding up and down hills has taken its toll. Glasses Chris was to take Goat Boy's Berlin entry. However, lost somewhere in the plethora of emails issued to all entrants was Goat Boy's registration document.

Consequently, any thoughts of relaxing with a bowl of pasta at yesterday's expo were to be abandoned. We spent well over an hour trying to track down Goat Boy back home in Brighton. The fact that he had been out on the lash on Thursday night, and was now too hung over to deal with such a crisis, did nothing to help our cause. The task of trawling through his email in-box was delegated to his P.A.* Despite her best efforts, Goat Boy's registration document was nowhere to be found. The officials at the expo agreed that Glasses Chris could be issued with his number if he could come back with some form of identification. Fortunately for him, several more of the guys were flying out here yesterday afternoon. This meant that we were able to get one of them to meet up with Goat Boy, once Goat Boy's hangover had subsided, and borrow his driving licence so that Glasses Chris could prove that he was, indeed, Goat Boy!

The slight problem with this plan was that Glasses Chris and Goat Boy bear no resemblance to each other. For example, Goat Boy doesn't wear glasses and Glasses Chris doesn't look like Tintin. However, I am pleased to confirm that our plan was somehow a success. The English got one over the Germans! Glasses Chris is in!

Despite the stress of our mini-crisis at the expo, my lasting memory of yesterday is, in fact, Glasses Chris's suitcase. Bearing in mind that he was 'between hotels', our day's sightseeing was accompanied by several hours of the dulcet drone of his baggage being wheeled up and down side streets, and through city centre and parkland. It is

**Goat Boy, after giving up running for Wales, went into the music industry. He now has his own, very successful, business, makes pots of cash and has a P.A. specifically employed to help him sort his life out.*

only now, some 30 hours later, that I'm beginning to get the noise out of my head... which is just as well, as my stress levels are starting to rise. It's not just that I'm a tad flustered about Fiona having taken Glasses Chris and me for a sightseeing walk almost far enough to be mistaken for a long Sunday training session, when I would have preferred to be resting, I am also a smidgeon concerned that my pre-race plan has taken me nearly twice as long to prepare as I expect to be running tomorrow morning.

Right, I think I'm finally there. 18 hours to go and my pre-race plan is complete....

5:50: Alarm.

5:51: Low G.I. Cereal.

5:55: Pint of Isotonic Drink.

6:00: Go back to bed.

6:45: Alarm again.

6:46: Shower.

7:00: Vaseline on nipples, toes and all moving parts.

7:03: Sun cream.

Not too much! Fiona has raised a concern, wondering if it might clog the pores and restrict the ability to sweat; you *need* to sweat, *I* need to sweat, I *am* sweating! I have to run 26.2 miles tomorrow at 9am!

In 2009, Fiona fainted 20 miles into the London Marathon and staggered home with Steve in 3 hours 33 minutes. However, a year later, having miscalculated her pacing by thinking that every 5 km was exactly 3 miles (us experienced runners know full well that 5 km is more like 3.1 miles), she ran far too fast and knocked out a ridiculous 2 hours 53 minutes. I'm now happy to take her advice. Steve, on the other hand, still needs to pull his finger out.

7:07: Put on shorts and vest.

Not socks, that's later as I have to apply anaesthetic gel to the ball of my right foot. This, of course, needs to be done before the socks go on and Nick said apply it an hour before the start. Well, this is clearly going to be impossible as we have to leave the hotel at 7:50 to walk to the start. Nick is a top-notch doctor / physiotherapist / god who I have kept in business for the last 15 years. I get a twinge, I call Nick. Acupuncture, bone crunching, epidurals, he loves it and, if at some point in my life it gets me a sub-3, so do I!

The reason for needing to apply anaesthetic gel to the ball of my right foot is because it hurts! In fact, just two weeks ago I had been contemplating pulling out of Berlin. A blister had formed, one so large I could have almost watered my favourite houseplant with the contents that spurted out when I popped it. Even after said popping, it was most uncomfortable to walk on and I was forced to refrain from running for three days.

7:10: 'Target pacing' bracelet on right wrist.

Now then, do I wear the '2 hour 56 minute' target pacing bracelet in preference to the '3 hour' target pacing bracelet, on the grounds that I'm going to go through half way in 1 hour 28 minutes?? (A 'target pacing' bracelet is nothing more than a strip of paper on which one's intended cumulative times at every kilometre are written, but a most useful monitoring tool to aid running at optimum pace.) After much deliberation, I think I'll go with the '3 hour' target pacing bracelet. That'll be preferential from a psychological standpoint when I consider that I may well not manage to maintain my intended '2 hour 56 minute' pace, thus free-falling into those oh-so-familiar depths of despair as I yet again fail miserably to run as well as I'd have liked. At least if I wear the '3 hour' target pacing bracelet and slip behind my planned '2 hour 56 minute' pace, I will still be able to observe with quiet confidence that I am ahead of schedule to cross the finish line in under 3 hours - which is what this is all about.

7:12: Gel belt around waist and gel band around left wrist.

Now this has been the most stressful part of the entire marathon build-up. Which energy gels to take, when, and how to carry them? From bitter and painful experience, I am all too aware that too many gels cause cramping by sapping moisture away from muscles. (I don't want another session in an ambulance as was the case after completing last year's Brighton Marathon.) Not enough and I'll be preparing for the dreaded wall! (Please refer to Glossary of Terms for 'The wall'.)

During my previous seven sub-3 marathon attempts, I have experimented with a variety of contraptions to carry sufficient fuel to get me through. I have yet to try running with a shopping basket but, quite frankly, I do not favour this approach. Of course, I could simply stuff the gels down my shorts. I tried this on one of my long Sunday runs but decided it wasn't for me just before I reached the front door on the way out. I do not fancy the idea of abrading my family allowance for over 26 miles.

Other gel-carrying methods have included simply holding in hands (cramp set in and it was some time after the finish that my fingers would properly separate), carrying in a bum bag (too cumbersome), stitching into shorts' waist band and also making use of a Velcro / plastic clip mechanism attached to the front and rear of my shorts. I think the latter two strategies would have been fine if I hadn't had to spend much of the morning clutching my shorts to prevent them falling to my ankles, owing to the enhanced weight they had clearly not been designed to accommodate.

7:15: Stick 'Breathe Right' strip on nose.

Anyone who knows me can't have escaped noticing that I have a rather large but narrow nose. Possibly less well known is my tendency to only breathe through my left nostril - not on purpose, you understand (inability-to-break-3-hours excuse no.27). I have never quite understood the merits of such nostril splaying as I generally inhale through my mouth when running. However, do not mock! If it brings world class status to Paula Radcliffe, then I am more than happy to decorate the front of my face with a piece of sticky tape and take all accompanying ridicule on the chin.

7:18: Put on Garmin.

This has been a major dilemma - to run with or without my Garmin?? It was only three months ago that I acquired my first Garmin, and it has been most helpful in letting me know, albeit in a somewhat insensitive manner, that I'm not as quick as I'd like to be. With a tendency to look at the damn thing far too frequently I risk adding valuable seconds (which I can ill afford) to my overall time, wearing out my left arm as it takes on the mindset of a yo-yo. I have decided to wear it - I just won't look at it too often. As an aside, I have found that it seems to wedge in place the energy gel that protrudes from the gel wrist band on my left wrist. Having taken into account the negative impact of the marginal additional weight, I think I have concluded that, in this regard, such a gel-flapping-reduction strategy can only be a good thing.

7:20: Anaesthetic gel to ball of right foot.

7:23: Put on socks.

Must be careful not to spread anaesthetic gel. I feel it important to retain some degree of sensation in my right foot.

7:25: Put on shoes.

Must make sure laces are not so tight as to bruise my tendons (as was the case a month ago, which stopped me running for four days), and not so loose as to encourage foot slippage and inevitable blistering. Blisters are no fun! Crikey, almost forgot my chip, which needs to be attached to one of my shoes. How disastrous would that be to complete my first ever sub-3 marathon and subsequently be disqualified for omitting to run with my chip!? This needs to go on my list of things to do today to save time tomorrow morning, along with charging Garmin, putting gel no.5 in shorts pocket and pinning race number to vest, taking particular care to ensure safety pins give nipples a suitably wide berth.

7:29: Beetroot shot.

Of course, this could be a completely pointless exercise as there's no telling whether drinking the purple dye is going to make me run any faster. I am told that its high nitrate content encourages increased blood flow and reduces the amount of oxygen needed by muscles. Only limited trials have been carried out to date, but I'm prepared to try anything if it means I'll cease to be categorised by Neil as a B-team jogger. As Neil smugly reminds me and my B-team jogger companions on a regular basis, he has knocked out a marathon in 2 hours 55 minutes. Well, that was a few years ago and tomorrow morning I'm going to beat him.

Actually, I was almost left beetroot-less as my Friday, Saturday and Sunday shots had, in fact, exploded in the baggage hold during my Thursday evening flight. I was somewhat relieved to find only minimal seepage, although you would not have thought so had you witnessed the state of my bag. On emptying it, my room began to resemble a murder scene, but I am hopeful that the subtle reduction in quantity of my pink-urine inducing beverage will not be too detrimental to my overall race performance.

For some inexplicable reason, Mark seems to have found great amusement in hearing about my near-catastrophe. He's a bit different to the rest of us. Abstaining from conventional running practices such as drills, stretching, having a rest day or gentle jog the day before a marathon, and choosing to dismiss all advice offered by physiotherapists, osteopaths and anyone associated with the medical profession, it would seem that his ability to churn out a marathon in 2 hours 49 minutes is attributed, in no small part, to a couple of visits to a faith healer and the wearing of a magnetic bracelet.

I appreciate that I am taking a huge risk in deciding not to follow Mark's sophisticated methodology. However, as already mentioned, there are several other accessories that I shall be attaching to my wrists. Not only would I struggle to find room for a magnetic bracelet, I would also have to consider the extra weight.

7:31: *Coffee.*

My mate Dave is one of Sussex's all-time finest distance runners with a 2:20 marathon to add to his list of jaw-dropping performances – and he drinks coffee like his life depends on it! Of course, caffeine isn't for everyone. It can cause stomach problems. A little bit late to be experimenting, but last Sunday on my 12-miler on Brighton seafront I took the opportunity to overdose on caffeine. Prior to the start, I drank a particularly strong cup of coffee – the equivalent of a treble espresso – and, during my 90-minute run, demolished three caffeinated energy gels. To complete the experiment, I then had a couple of post-run cappuccinos. In conclusion, although I struggled to enjoy an afternoon nap that day, I suffered no stomach problems and therefore I can see no harm in having a small coffee at 7:31 tomorrow morning, (as well as a couple of caffeine-laced gels in the second half of the race).

7:33: Brush teeth.

7:35: Remain in bathroom and lose weight.

7:45: Check out of hotel and dump suitcase behind reception desk (for collection after a post-marathon celebratory German beer or two en route to airport in running kit).

7:50: Put on hat and commence slow leisurely walk to the start, remaining chilled, calm and focused.

8:00: Arrive at start.

8:20: Dump race bag (needs to be done by 8:30 at the latest).

8:35: Short warm-up and gentle stretching (as close to the start as possible).

8:50: Get into starting pen.

It is normally at this point that I begin jumping up and down as if on an invisible pogo stick, excitement boiling over and burning up valuable glycogen stores supplied by several days' ingestion of fusilli, penne, tagliatelle, spaghetti and various other shapes of all-important durum wheat. Tomorrow, however, I shall remain totally stationary, not so much as batting an eyelid, so as to conserve every morsel of energy required for the three hours of tarmac pounding to follow.

8:52: Lob empty energy drink bottle to side of road.

Must be careful to avoid striking any young children on the head.

8:59: Right forefinger into position, hovering over start button on Garmin. Lean forward slightly. Await gun.

So, there we have it, a pre-race plan, my first ever pre-race plan. I'm organised. I'm prepared. This is the year. This is my race. For all the doubters, for all those who have believed in me, for myself, for my sanity, for my children, for my grandchildren*, to be etched in history for ever and never taken away from me, tomorrow morning I'm going to break 3 hours.

**It might be worth mentioning that I don't actually have any grandchildren. In fact, come to think of it, I don't have any children either. But if one day I do, well, I guess it would be a nice touch if this were, in part, for them!*

Chapter 2

Thermometers up Rectums

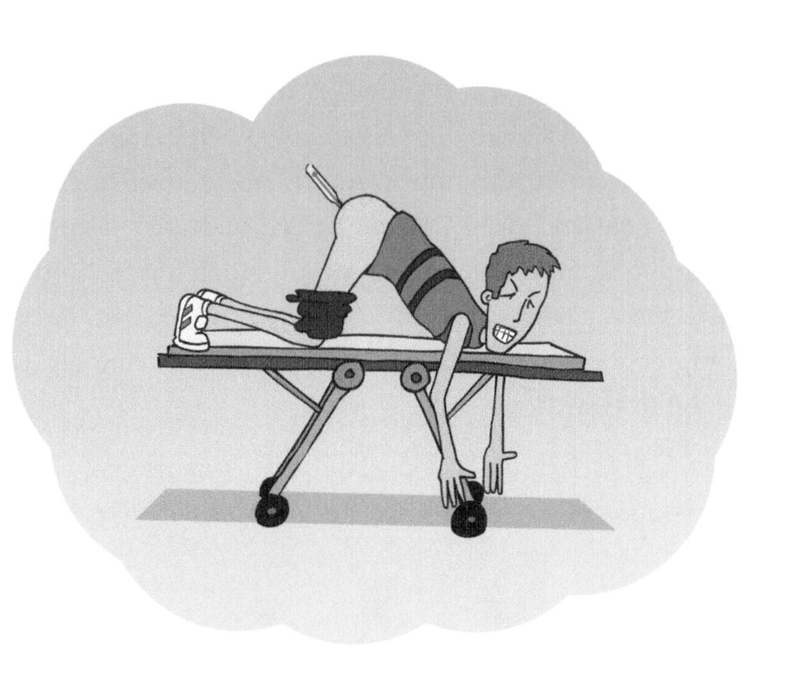

Of course, it's about much more than having a pre-race plan.

Unfortunately, featuring relatively high on the marathon preparation list is the need to train. As much as I would love to show up at the start line after a few jogs around the block and, 179 minutes later, be able to tick the 'been-there-done-that' box, we all know this just isn't going to happen. And whilst it is generally considered advisable to bang out more mileage than you would if you were simply getting ready for an egg-and-spoon race, there's a bit more to training than chalking up the miles. Tempo runs, recovery jogs, lactate threshold runs, hill reps, $V0_2$ max sessions... the list goes on. And that's just the running. Then there's the strength training, the flexibility training, core stability exercises, plyometrics and cross training. Add to this mix concerns about over-training, what to eat and drink before, during and after training, returning from injury, how to avoid getting injured in the first place, what type of shoes to wear, orthotics, compression socks, massage..... who said that running is straightforward?!

There's lots I can tell you about my own training and preparation but, bear with me, I'll come back to that later.

So, with the training now behind me and most of the items on my pre-race plan successfully ticked off, my running mates and I leave the hotel and wander to the start. On arrival, it becomes immediately apparent that there's going to be a degree of chaos in fighting through dense crowds to find our respective baggage tents. One might have expected that the baggage tent for running numbers 1 - 4000 would have been vaguely in the vicinity of the

4001 - 8000 tent, etc. However, this does not appear to be so. I begin to wonder if I have entered an orienteering event. We wish each other luck and promptly split up to go our separate ways in search of our tents.

I eventually drop off my bag. It's time to make for the starting pen with no more than a 3-minute jog warm-up at walking pace with the surrounding herds, stopping off briefly in the adjacent woodland for a last minute pee. Not ideal, but nonetheless somewhat more beneficial, I suspect, than my mate Roger's* classic warm-up routine of remaining seated in his car with the heater on, whilst sipping tea and eating a bacon sandwich.

At 8:50, I am in my pen and raring to get started. Using my height to peer over a sea of heads, I am able to observe the wide, flat tarmac road stretching out into the distance in front of me. Some of the world's finest marathoners are striding up and down, carrying out their final preparations for what potential achievements lie ahead. Amongst them, both current world record holders – Ethiopia's Haile Gebrselassie and our very own Paula

** Roger, like Mark, has never done any stretching in his life. (Nor, for that matter, has his dad, who used to run for GB and still, at over 80 years of age, runs over 70 miles a week.) Roger's principal marathon prep, just hours before a race, tends to be a session of nightclubbing and drinking something like 11 pints of beer, half a bottle of wine and a couple of gin and tonics. I'm not sure Roger has ever quite reached his potential.*

Radcliffe. Their presence is introduced over the loudspeakers and we 33,000 slower runners applaud in awe of such tremendous athletes.

I am now to put these elites out of my head until well after the finish and concentrate, through to just shy of mid-day, on my own far more important mission. I check that all my energy gels are where they are supposed to be, crouch to re-tie my laces just to be sure they are at the optimum tension, then check again to make sure my gels are still where they are supposed to be (just in case they have fallen off or have been stolen at some point in the preceding 30 seconds whilst my attentions were focused on shoelace tying). Tilting my head from side to side and gently rolling my shoulders, I treat my neck to a last little stretch. I adjust my hat, glance at my Garmin to check the screen is correctly displaying a row of zeros and, with forefinger in position, I am ready - a damn sight more ready than I was for the Seaford 10k, still on the toilet when the starting gun was fired.

I don't feel it necessary to say any more about the Seaford 10k - apart from the fact that I came 16th and am reasonably confident that I would have finished in the top 15 had I not been on the toilet when the starting gun was fired!

The decision to enter Berlin was made 11 months ago. There had been some exchange of email banter which began with Mark's proposition to return to this historic city, to not only beat his personal best time of 2:49 which was set there last year, but to go for sub-2:45. As we all know, Berlin offers a flat and fast course on which world records have been broken. Tempting! I ran 3:03 in Brighton last year and came away from it clearly identifying factors I believed could be improved upon.

I had enjoyed running Brighton more than the six Londons which preceded it, despite the day being quite hot and the course containing a couple of climbs. There were several positive factors that made this seaside marathon so special, not least that it was on home territory. The support the whole way round was fantastic as friends yelled encouragement from the sidelines throughout the entire course. A group of us donning our red and black Brighton & Hove Athletics Club vests stuck together until well beyond the half way mark, our colours being spotted from afar as we came into view of excited fellow Brightonians.

The constant wave of encouragement provided a huge on-going source of energy. However, there is a limit to how far such support can carry you as the body fatigues. At about 15 miles I was a couple of seconds off the pace and found it hard to maintain position for the next 5 miles, but dug deep and was able to hold on. I was confident, with

10 km remaining, that I would be able to find the inner strength required to fight and claw back the minute or so lost between miles 15 and 20. I'm a strong finisher. There's another gear, come on, I can do this. I could hear Mark's voice repeatedly telling me as he had in training, "It's all in your head!" I agreed. It was all in my head. It certainly wasn't in my legs. I pushed on, convincing myself that my weakened legs were just in my imagination. By mile 23, my calves were screaming. I maintained pace, but it was not much further down the road that the pain told me I would once again fail to crack 3 hours. Keep going! Keep going! If I hang on, I can beat my 3:02 PB, which was set nine years ago. Legs buckling beneath me, I couldn't hide the pain. The next two miles seemed like an eternity. Several times during the final mile my legs almost abandoned me. I somehow remained on my feet until I staggered over the finish line where I collapsed to the ground.

I had finished in 3 hours 3 minutes 13 seconds.

It hadn't been my day. No sub-3, not even a PB. And as my whole body descended into shock I spent the next 3 hours with the medics. Lying in the back of an ambulance, with a thermometer up my arse, I began to question whether marathon running was for me. What had gone wrong? I set about the habitual process of analysis, a process that would occupy most of my thoughts in the coming week, trying to figure out what was to blame for yet another failure, leaving me still unqualified to join the sub-3 club. Was there one principal reason, or were there several contributory factors? Was it down to lack of training, the wrong type of training, the wrong energy gels, too many gels, the heat, the wrong choice of shoe, the wrong type of orthotic, not drinking enough water??? I'm fairly confident it wasn't down to a lack of carbo-loading; since Wednesday morning, I'd chomped my way through 18 bowls of pasta!

Whatever the reason, right now it didn't matter. No sub-3! No PB! Still a B-team jogger!

My core temperature returned to normal and I was released from the ambulance.

That evening in the Market Inn, medals were worn with pride and stories were exchanged – stories of PB marathons, debut marathons, praise for the organisers, praise for the supporters, high points, low points, split times, injuries, the exact location of 'the wall' and thermometers up rectums. We all had our own personal stories and experiences, but one thing united us - we had all just run a marathon.

During the days that followed, every time I attempted to stand, sit or walk, my legs constantly reminded me that I had just run 26 miles and 385 yards as hard as I possibly could have. I had not held back. I had given it my all. The only way to lower myself onto the lavatory was by strangling the radiator with my right arm and almost ripping the basin off the wall with my left. My quads screamed with disapproval and, after completing my ablutions, I had to lie down for 10 minutes to get my breath back. In my local supermarket, a pensioner helped me to my feet when I over-exerted myself reaching for something on the bottom shelf and found myself stranded on the floor.

After about five days, some degree of normality resumed and I was soon able to lower myself unaided onto the toilet. Having had time to reflect, I identified some areas for improvement in my next embarkation on sub-3.

Having run Brighton in 3:03:13, I only needed to improve by 1.8%. Surely, finding a flat course would go a fair way to narrowing the gap and, as long as I didn't choose a mid-summer marathon, cooler conditions would definitely help further.

I carried out some research on energy gels and concluded that I had taken too many in Brighton. I had taken six of the gloopy ones, which are predominantly carbohydrate. Although I drank water with them, it seems I should have drunk far more, as they have a tendency to sap moisture from muscles, and cause cramp. What I should have taken on (apparently) was more isotonic fuel, the purpose of which (apparently) is to replace salts and minerals lost through sweating, particularly when running in the heat.

Losing such salts and minerals is (apparently) another major cause of cramping. If addressing this issue would stop me cramping, I'd be able to run pain-free for longer and my legs wouldn't seize up (apparently)!

And so as not to rely on a flat course on a cool day and simply improve my fuelling strategy, I also decided to up my weekly mileage.

I recalled Albert Einstein's quote regarding the definition of insanity: "Doing the same thing over and over again and expecting different results". I knew full well that I couldn't simply run another marathon and hope to be faster than last time. After all, I was also getting older! I had to identify areas for improvement and I was confident I had done this.

Most importantly, in preparation for Berlin, I have, for the first time, followed a comprehensive training programme. This might sound like a bizarre declaration from someone who has been training for, and competing in, marathons for 15 years, but it occurred to me that I hadn't previously been guided by any specific, detailed training programme. I realised that, in the past, my choice of sessions was determined by taking a variety of tips from experienced runners and then, with no particular rationale, attempting to string them all together in a manner that simply hasn't worked.

So, on this occasion, I have adopted one of the training schedules set out in *Advanced Marathoning* by Pete Pfitzinger and Scott Douglas. I was introduced to this most helpful book by my friend Cathy.

Cathy is able to boast many running-related attributes. The most notable of these is her ability to cause car drivers to crash as a result of being distracted by her slender figure and rather skimpy running attire.

Last year, at the ripe old age of 47 and in a time of 3 hours 5 minutes, Cathy was the first Brighton woman home in the inaugural Brighton Marathon - and second woman overall. That, to me, is a pretty awesome achievement. I took the view that I wouldn't go far wrong if I followed the same programme as Cathy, so I got myself a copy of *Advanced Marathoning* and decided to give Pfitzinger and Douglas's training schedule a shot.

So now, to put what I have learned to the test! I shall know in 3 hours' time whether this programme has worked. I can say with confidence, though, that I have emerged having acquired a wealth of knowledge of the multitude of factors that (apparently) constitute thorough marathon preparation.

A few hundred metres behind me the historic and beautiful Brandenburg Gate stands proud, watching over me as if to wave me off and wish me well as I head into battle, with the promise that she will be waiting for my return.

I vow to be back before mid-day but can't swear to return unscathed. The journey won't be easy. I can't predict how long I shall remain in my comfort zone - probably beyond mid-way, hopefully to at least 20 miles - but one thing is for sure, at some stage I shall need to fight. My tiring body will come to be in conflict with my mind – a battle of wits – and my head will need to take over for the latter stages in this conquest. Any feelings of discomfort, depletion of energy, pain and overwhelming need to stop and give up will have to be overruled by utter determination and the will to succeed.

I shall be returning strong into the arms of the Brandenburg Gate no later than 11:58 am, with a rush of adrenaline to carry me the final few hundred metres to glory and adulation.

The starting gun is fired.

Chapter 3
Meeting Haile

In the back of my mind, I recall a quote from Haile (the little fella at the front who holds the world record): "No race begins at the start line!" Tom, Cathy, Richard and I had debated the meaning of this as we caught the bus back from Heathrow following our trip to Ethiopia. It was the inscription on the toothpick wrappers in the restaurant of Haile's hotel, the Haile Resort in Hawassa. We concluded that there were two interpretations. The race could begin months earlier when training commences (or arguably years earlier as it can take a lifetime of running to reach one's personal best). Otherwise, the reference could relate to running comfortably for a major part of the event on the actual day, sticking together as a group before someone decides to make the break and pull away from the pack - perhaps it is at that moment that the race begins?

Both interpretations carried weight.

Tom, many moons ago when he was young, completed a marathon in 2 hours 27 minutes. In fact, most impressively, he has continued to maintain form over the decades and has run a sub-3 marathon in his 20's, 30's and 40's. Sadly, injury has denied him a line-up at the start today, age 55, but I am confident we'll be seeing a sub-3 from Tom at some point in the current decade.

In May 2002 on the Green Belt Relay, a fantastic running event that takes in the surprisingly scenic countryside on a course not too far from the M25 motorway, Tom was introduced to Cathy. Tom and Cathy were soon to become 'Tom and Cathy' and, a year later at the same annual event, he proposed marriage. Another year on, they were hitched! A large group of us get together each year for the Tom & Cathy 10-miler on Brighton seafront to celebrate their anniversary.

As for Richard, well, in the mid 1990s he was Britain's best. With a win in the World Cup Marathon in San Sebastian in 1993, 5th place in the Olympic Marathon in Atlanta in 1996 and a personal best time of 2 hours 8 minutes, the concept of someone taking 15 years to break 3 hours must seem rather alien. Richard now resides in Brighton but for many years lived in Ethiopia and is great pals with Haile.

I was introduced to Richard at a launch event for the Brighton Half Marathon after hearing talk about a trip to Ethiopia. A keen traveller, always up for visiting somewhere new and interesting, my ears pricked up. At the mention of getting to meet his mate Haile, I was sold.

A few months later, four of us from Brighton (Tom, Cathy, Fiona and I) were off to catch a flight to Addis Ababa for a five-day trip, the highlight of which would be to run the 'Haile Half' (Hawassa Half Marathon). We would be staying at the Haile Resort and meeting the great man himself.

For me, though, this was no conventional race; in fact it was not really a race at all. I hadn't run properly in ages. Having over-indulged on my birthday three months earlier, oblivious to a chest infection that was waiting to pounce, and then totally zapping my immune system with a 15-mile hangover run the next morning, I had swiftly plunged into a month of illness.

My birthday night had been a hoot, a fairly low key evening with the hardcore of Brighton friends, David, Helena*, Cathy, Tom, Fiona and myself all consuming not an insignificant quantity of champagne, Guinness and red wine. A most entertaining occasion, the highlights being when David, habitually placid (excepting the time that he raced the 400m hurdles, naked), was almost thrown out of the Black Lion for dancing on a table, and some random person setting the evening alight as her hair caught fire when she inadvertently leant back against a rather tall candle. Marvellous! We all subsequently became ill and were unable to compete in various races which we had already entered and paid for. With Fiona, Helena and me targeting a PB at the Eastleigh 10k, our lurgy was later nicknamed the 'Eastleigh Bug'. In fact, as I had been planning on running the second Brighton Marathon just a few weeks later, this was yet another on a long list of illnesses / injuries that prevented me from making it to the start line.

On eventual return to health, my legs felt great, having benefited from a month's rest. I thought it sensible to begin with no more than a 5 km run. However, unable to

**Helena is a former medallist in the UK Indoor Championships for both 800m and 1500m, but she's never run a marathon! Her brother Rob represents Great Britain in the 4 x 400m and is a strong believer in beetroot shots! On a night out in Brighton, I once challenged him to a race between a couple of lampposts. He declined. I win!*

be completely sensible, I ran too quickly and strained a calf muscle. It was another week before I could go for so much as a gentle jog. Second time around, I figured I'd just run a slow mile or two every other day. By the time I was able to progress beyond a short slow jog, there remained only a fortnight before I was to run 13.1 miles at altitude in Hawassa; hence deciding upon the objective of completing the course rather than racing it.

There were 15 of us from the UK in total, and Richard introduced us all to each other as we converged at Heathrow. As the group of us, in the range 'jogger to elite', exchanged banter in the departure lounge, we learned of which club each of us represented and how quickly each of us might expect to get around the course, and discovered unsurprising mutual excitement about meeting the greatest runner of all time – an excitement bolstered by the relief of being able to escape a royal wedding occupying the entire UK media.

Frustratingly for me, I found myself being introduced to yet more runners who have had no problem whatsoever in running their marathons in under 3 hours.

Before we could enter the country, we had to get ourselves through Customs in Addis. This was never going to be straightforward. We queued for the best part of an hour to submit our immigration cards and have our passports scrutinised before being stamped.

Once that complex task was complete, there was the small matter of the self-inflicted suspicion that we aroused by bringing 24 boxes into the country, each of which contained five bottles of biological reagents.

Richard's wife, Gail, is a doctor and medical research scientist, currently at Brighton & Sussex Medical School, having previously worked for nine years at Addis Ababa University. Our trip provided an ideal opportunity to take out much sought-after laboratory reagents for a medical research group working in collaboration with Gail. However, as the Ethiopian immigration authorities looked over the boxes, they seemed to eye us up and down as if convinced that we were trying to import illegal drugs. After much deliberation by the authorities, we were permitted to proceed and enter the country; our 24 boxes were not - at least, not with us and not that day. They were to remain with Customs for several days, to be analysed before the recipient scientist was allowed to come by and take our delivery off their hands.

Gail's principal research focus is on a disease, little known in the Western world, called podoconiosis, a form of elephantiasis otherwise known as Mossy Foot. Its primary manifestation is swelling and often extreme deformity of the lower legs and feet. It is thought to be caused by particles in the distinctive red clay that exists throughout tropical Africa.

Ethiopia is the worst affected country on the continent. A staggering 5% of the population in endemic areas suffer from podoconiosis and this typically results in severe physical disability compounded by the inability to work, as well as the psychological effects of social stigma. With the suspected link to walking barefoot, it is hard to comprehend that such widespread disability could be prevented by simply affording to buy shoes. And it is somewhat ironic that so many people are crippled by this appalling disease in a country that produces some of the world's finest athletes.

Closer to home, in the last couple of years there has been much debate about the pros and cons of running-shoe technology versus the principles of barefoot running. Some would argue that our natural running style involves landing predominantly on the forefoot, whereas our running shoes have been developed in such a way as to provide a significant amount of cushioning under the heel. The barefoot running advocates suggest that we have become reliant on the rear foot cushioning and have consequently adopted a lazy running style involving more of a heel strike. This, they would contest, is a fundamental cause of many running injuries. On the grounds that my entire circle of running friends are forever picking up injuries and we all run in shoes, perhaps there is some weight in the barefoot argument.

Having stated the above, many of my training routes are on the South Downs which, as you might expect, involves running through fields of cow dung and sheep droppings and along farm tracks where horses have no qualms about relieving themselves in the middle of my path whenever they feel like it. I think, for the time being, to avoid shit from our four-legged friends clogging up in between my toes and getting compacted under my nails, call me old-fashioned but I'll be keeping my shoes on.

Walking out into the warm air that enveloped Addis airport early on this Friday morning, the city in front of me appeared far more developed than I had been anticipating and seemed to be undergoing a considerable amount of construction in progress. Nothing like a city in any quarter of a Westernised society, but nonetheless more advanced than I had previously seen in Africa.

Our five-day round trip was going to be rather full-on. Not only was there the small matter of running a half marathon at altitude, there would also be a significant amount of time spent on a bus, some sightseeing and an introduction to Ethiopian way of life.

We checked in at the Beer Garden Hotel and wasted no time in heading for the dining room for breakfast just moments before it was to be packed away. We were offered the usual choice of tea or coffee. Of course, as we were in Ethiopia, the original home of the coffee plant, it had to be coffee! And it was the strongest cup of coffee I had ever tasted. It was almost a case of eating it rather than drinking it. I certainly wouldn't be nodding off during the morning's sightseeing.

After breakfast, we boarded a minibus and, accompanied by our guide, Fasica, headed for the Entoto Mountains and St Mary's Church. The large open area in front of the church is a regular meeting place for early-morning runners. Unfortunately we couldn't enter St Mary's because it was St Mary's Day! A large group of children were playing in front of the entrance and were intrigued as to what we were up to. We were also intrigued as to why all these children weren't in school. It seems it was a holiday. When we explained that we were runners and that we were going to be meeting Haile Gebrselassie, their eyes lit up with excitement. They all knew who Haile was. It was becoming clear to me that Haile is not just respected throughout the world of athletics, in Ethiopia he is a national hero.

Continuing on our bus, we climbed further into the mountains. This is a popular training ground for Haile and other Ethiopian runners, elite or otherwise. Fuelled by the caffeine consumed at breakfast, a few of us decided to pop on our running shoes and test out our lungs on our debut jog at altitude*. Again, we found ourselves surrounded by local children who, just like those outside St Mary's, were dressed in a mesmerising mis-matched concoction of garments, all seemingly belonging to taller siblings. I broke into a jog along the mountain road and into the bordering forest and, breathing hard to inhale the thin air, promptly found myself being overtaken by a group of kids, led by a 10-year-old in a purple suit.

At the end of the morning we headed back on our bus down towards Addis and for lunch at Lucy's Restaurant, situated next door to the National Museum. It is in this museum that Lucy's skeleton is displayed. Leaving aside Haile for a moment, Lucy is the most famous person in Ethiopia. In 1974, several hundred pieces of hominid bone were discovered - an amazing find, representing a significant proportion of the remains of an individual said to have lived over three million years ago, pre-dating any other such discovery. She was given her name by the anthropologist who discovered her. With his expedition crew who had sat around in the evenings listening to

**It occurred to me that something I've not yet tried in my quest to break 3 hours is spending some time living at altitude. However, I have to draw the line somewhere. Unfortunately I have a job – I can't just up-sticks and go and live in Ethiopia for six months. Well... actually... I suppose I shouldn't rule this out?*

Beatles songs, it was agreed she would be named after the song 'Lucy in the sky with diamonds'.

The centrepiece of our lunch was a rather intriguing vegetable root with a texture not too dissimilar to chamois leather. This speciality, called 'injera', is a traditional dish eaten with an assortment of side dishes.

There was more 'chamois leather' eating to be had that evening, which was spent in Elfign, a delightful traditional restaurant a short walk from our hotel. Entertainment came in the form of some fascinating dancing. It incorporated a rather interesting movement of heads from side to side as if detached from the shoulders on which they oscillated. One of our group, Martin from Grantham*, needed no encouragement to participate. Within minutes of the dancers taking to the stage he briefly disappeared around the back, then re-appeared in full regalia, blending in perfectly with the ensuing routine as if Ethiopian dancing had been a regularly practised pastime.

At breakfast the following morning, alone at one of the tables in the dining room sat a young man of slight build and darker skin than that of the Ethiopians we had met so far. Richard had told us that an elite Kenyan runner had been invited to take part in the Haile Half and would be

**I don't know much about Martin from Grantham, other than he updates Facebook with the split times of his training runs more than I do... and that he's run a marathon comfortably inside 3 hours.*

joining us on our bus to Hawassa. With the tiny physique typical of African distance runners, there were pretty good odds that this chap was our Kenyan athlete.

A short while later we boarded our bus. This would take us through just a small part of the vast barren landscape of the Rift Valley on our way to Hawassa.

Sure enough, the little fella we'd clocked at breakfast was on our bus. I moved down from my seat at the rear to introduce myself. He was sitting next to an Ethiopian gentleman, also of athletic build.

It transpired that the Kenyan was Kiplimo Kimutai, whose many great achievements include 2nd place to Martin Lel in the 2008 Great North Run, 2nd place to Haile in the 2009 Great North Run, and 1st place in the 2007 & 2008 Hastings Half Marathons.

The Ethiopian who was accompanying him was Assefa Mezgebu, bronze medallist in the 10,000m at the Sydney Olympics.

I was Mike Bannister, the only runner to date who has managed to win Hove parkrun* in over 20 minutes. Neither of them had heard of me. I explained that my

**parkrun is an increasingly popular weekly event involving a 5 km run, which takes place in numerous locations around the world. Paul Sinton-Hewitt, the founder of parkrun, will no doubt be appalled by my mention of a win. Apparently it's a run, not a race, which means I didn't actually win, I came first!*

greatest ever victory had taken place in the snow at Christmas when the majority of the regulars had gone home. I was surprised at their obliviousness as my result had been noted in Athletics Weekly.

A couple of hours into our drive, having successfully negotiated numerous goats and donkeys who seemed to take priority over all other road users, our driver pulled over to allow us a 15-minute toilet break.

I continued to interrogate Kippy in the queue for a hole in the ground. I was intrigued as he explained to me in broken English that he had once won a red car. "What a fantastic prize for winning a race!", I said. "I once won a £20 Jog Shop voucher for coming second in the annual Brighton Trailblazer on the South Downs." (It had previously been a 'girls only' race; the year I came second was the first year it was opened up to male runners, except not many males knew about it and only half a dozen of us turned up.)

Kippy looked at me blankly.

I later discovered that he had not actually won a red car; he had won Redcar, as in the Redcar Half Marathon - oh, and broken the course record.

We continued on our journey and, as lunchtime approached, we turned off the main road for Lake Langano. We were greeted by some of the local village children. They were doing handstands in the road in front of our bus as if performing some kind of welcoming ritual. Others came up to the side of the bus trying to sell us their hand-made wooden souvenirs through the windows.

We politely declined their offers and proceeded to make our way to a restaurant overlooking the lake.

There was an exceptionally long wait for lunch, but we made best use of the time by taking in the beautiful views across the lake and enjoying a surreal conversation with Kiplimo and Assefa. Fiona showed them her copy of '*Haile Gebrselassie - The greatest runner of all time*' by Klaus Weidt. At the back of the book there is a list of Haile's numerous world records. Assefa pointed out to us that he had, in fact, paced Haile in several of those record races. There is an interview featured in the book where Haile is asked if he could recall any particular low points in his otherwise incredibly successful running career. He explained that he had been most disappointed with his third place in the World Championship 10,000m race in Edmonton in 2001. Assefa, it transpired, had nipped ahead of him for silver!

Some eight hours after leaving Addis we checked into the Haile Resort, went for a brief run along the first part of the half marathon course, and then jumped in a tuc-tuc to downtown Hawassa where Richard would introduce us to Mr Gebrselassie.

The square was packed with locals, never tiring of seeing their national hero. The event was a promotion of the

Every One Campaign, which had been selected as the recipient charity of the 'Haile Half' profits. Great Ethiopian Run, the organisation that stages the Haile Half and other running events in Ethiopia, has an ethos for raising funds for essential causes in the form of health campaigns.

From what we could gather, the evening in Hawassa revolved around a quiz regarding the multitude of achievements of Ethiopia's no.1 runner. From the stage, no words were spoken in English, but Richard, conversant in Amharic, helped us to understand what was going on. I suspect that everyone in attendance knew that Haile held the world marathon record in a time of 2:03:59, but I bet none of them could provide any explanation as to why, after training for 15 years, the lanky white guy at the back couldn't get within 58 minutes of him. I was intrigued by the hold that Haile had on his attentive audience, all trying to get as close as possible to the great man. We would have to wait a little longer before it was convenient for Richard to introduce us to his world-famous mate.

I was finally introduced to Haile, shook his hand and was immediately lost for words. I think his permanent beaming smile had cast a spell on me. He was joking around, suggesting that we had come to visit Ethiopia at the wrong time - it was pre-monsoon season, which meant that the preceding long dry spell would not permit us to marvel at the beautiful lush green landscape that we might have enjoyed had we deferred our trip to later in the year. All very well, but the Haile Half was taking place the next day. I didn't feel it was my place to suggest he move the event to a different date. Thanks to Richard, for a moment we had Haile's attention. As Haile chatted with us, Richard assumed the role of bodyguard and did his best to protect his mate from being bombarded by swarms of fans, then helped clear a way to enable Haile to get to his waiting car.

Despite Richard's 2:08 making him one of the fastest British marathoners of all time, I couldn't help but wonder if, in Haile's presence, he considers himself a mere jogger.

I felt privileged to have been in Haile's company, if only for a minute. And yet, I felt a clear sense that he also enjoys the celebrity status. Unless it's just an act, which I very much doubt, it's as though he'd be happy chatting with fans, signing autographs and having his photograph taken all day long. A long way for us to have travelled to meet our hero, but it was worth it - it's not every day you get to shake the hand of someone who has broken 27 world records!

We returned to the hotel for dinner and guess who should be dining on the next table! I think he was stalking us, probably trying to earwig our conversation in order to pick up some race tips. Before we knew it, he was over having his photo taken with us. I think someone had told him about my Hove parkrun victory! The truth was, excepting our photo session, Haile seemed to spend the entire time with his mobile phone glued to his ear. He is not just at the top of the world of athletics, but also has interests in numerous business ventures which, of course, involve being constantly in communication to ensure he doesn't miss a trick.

It was getting late. We allowed Haile to concentrate on his own affairs, as we turned our attention to the half marathon.

In order to avoid running in the high temperatures that we would undoubtedly begin to experience from mid-morning, the race was scheduled to commence at the very unsociable time of 6:30am. This meant we would need to have had breakfast by 5am latest. No late night tonight then! Time for bed!

As is so often the case, I sped off from the start line far too quickly.

I was pleased to keep up with Cathy and Tom for the first half, but then I began to tire and was reminded of my objective to complete the course rather than race it.

Countless people overtook me as I slowed to take in the beautiful scenery of Lake Hawassa to my right and a squadron of pelicans to my left. I 'high-fived' excited children at the roadside, their infectious giggling delivering ripples of energy to carry me through the last few miles.

I caught up with a chap called Nibret from Addis who was competing in his first half marathon. He was tiring even more than I was. We got chatting and spurred each other on, completing the last 15-minute stretch together. I felt good, particularly when I later discovered that he was part of the first placed team. No prizes for me that day. What I got for completing the course was far more special than any trophy. To my complete surprise, Haile was there to shake my hand as I crossed the line.

Moments later, I discovered that Fiona was the winning girl and Cathy was second. Fantastic! The men's winner was Andrew, one of the 15 of us from the UK we had got to know over the last couple of days.

All of our times were significantly down on our PBs, but we had expected that. As anticipated, we had all been clearly affected by the altitude. I had not come all this way for a PB, but rather this was one of the most enjoyable of all my running experiences.

So, that was the mass race. The elite race commenced as Nibret and I spurted down the home straight.

We wandered back out on to the course to watch the elites come in. There were 79 Ethiopians and one Kenyan in the elite men's race. You can imagine how thrilled we were to see our newfound friend, Kippy the Kenyan, striding out to victory with a new course record!

As Tom and I slowly shrivelled up in the mid-morning sun, awaiting the presentation ceremony, the winners amongst us (Fi, Cathy, Andrew, Kiplimo, Nibret *et al*) were able to remain cool in the tented area adjacent to the stage. A huge crowd of children pushed forward, excited that their hero, Haile, would at some point in the next hour be on stage to present the awards. Tom and I held our ground; we would not have been forgiven if we hadn't managed to get photographs of Fi and Cathy being handed their awards by the man himself..... We got our photos and headed back to the hotel.

I managed to squeeze in a couple of games of table tennis before lunch.

Lunch was amazing - a fantastic outdoor buffet, followed by speeches from, amongst others, Richard and Haile. Their speeches revolved around not just the tremendous success of the Haile Half but also a reminder of the tremendously important work of the Every One Campaign. Haile also pointed out, albeit in good spirit, how peeved he was that none of his fellow Ethiopians had managed to beat the only Kenyan in the race!

Our time in Hawassa and our stay at the Haile Resort had been brief, far too brief; it was time for our eight hour bus ride back to Addis.

On our eventual arrival back at the Beer Garden Hotel, our group of 15, plus Kiplimo, enjoyed our last meal together in the hotel bar.

All too quickly, the following morning came around and it was time to depart. I found myself chatting to Hugh Jones who, in 1982, took it upon himself to win the London Marathon. Hugh travels around the world taking responsibility for ensuring race course distances are accurately measured. In fact, that was why he was in Ethiopia. Richard had arranged for him to check the length of the Hawassa course - as well as perform the role of lead bike. He proceeded to explain that, at one point, the leaders had gone the wrong way, causing him to make a sharp turn and fall off his bike. I could relate to his embarrassment as I once flinched and fell off my bike when a school friend shot me with a pea shooter. I realised that Hugh and I had a couple of things in common. Not only had we both experienced tumbling from our bicycles in a humiliating fashion, we were also able to hold a sensible conversation about measuring techniques as in the late 1980s I had a job as a setting-out engineer.

Hugh was yet another proper runner whom I'd had the privilege to meet on my trip to Ethiopia. It was obvious that we shared the same passion; it's just that these guys are all a damn sight more talented than I am and no doubt totally baffled as to why, after 15 years, I'm still unable to run a marathon in '2 something'! We said our goodbyes to our fantastic host and guide, Fasica, and at the airport made Kippy promise to come and stay with us next time he was racing in the UK.

Chapter 4

Norbel

The time has come to temporarily part company with the Brandenburg Gate. Following the sound of the gun, 33,000 of us ease away from the start line, which has taken me just 18 seconds to reach. The first kilometre is slow but that's ok, I have been prepared for that. In an attempt to avoid bunching up too close to those around me, so as not to tread on anyone's heels or have my own heels trodden on (and, more crucially, to minimise the possibility of my gels being dislodged), I spend the first couple of minutes with my arms out wide, adopting such a posture as if to be bear-hugging the invisible man. If it is this crowded so close to the front, it wouldn't surprise me if the leaders complete 10 km by the time those at the rear get through the start.

I spent much of yesterday sitting in a cafe, deliberating over my race strategy and determining my optimal pacing. I have taken advice from many experienced marathoners and am still none the wiser.

Some would recommend 'negative splits', completing the second half of the race very slightly faster than the first half, the theory being that overall less energy is expended when compared with running a faster first half. I have tried adopting this strategy in some of my previous marathons, getting through the first 13.1 miles in a smidgeon outside 90 minutes, only to hit the dreaded wall somewhere between 18 and 24 miles, fizzle out, and complete the second 13.1 miles a fair bit outside 90 minutes.

Other equally experienced marathoners would insist on the importance of getting through half way in a bit less than half of one's overall target time. The rationale behind the latter approach is supported by some scientific reasoning. For the majority of a marathon we use our slow-twitch muscle fibres, until our glycogen stores become depleted. We then switch to using our fast-twitch muscle fibres, which are less efficient, so we slow down. I have applied this logic to other of my marathons and set out to run the first half in times varying from 1:26 to 1:29. It hasn't worked!

Having dedicated an inordinate amount of time during the last few weeks considering these conflicting views, I have concluded that this morning, in Berlin, I will run at 4 minutes 10 seconds per kilometre, excepting the first kilometre, which I shall run in 4:20. The 4:20 first kilometre will prevent me going off too quickly, and with the next 20 km at 4:10, this will get me through half way in 1 hour 28 minutes 5 seconds. From half way, I shall continue at 4:10 pace for as long as I can hold on, affording me 21 minutes for the final 5 km. Well, I have run a 5 km race in 17:36 so, all things considered, this ought to be achievable.

So far, so good; first kilometre completed in 4:22 - two seconds off pace. I can live with that. I feel good, bags of energy, but it's still quite crowded – surely the hundreds of runners boxing me in don't all plan to run at an identical pace. I need some space. I'm beginning to feel just a tad claustrophobic. I need to drop the bear-hug pose.

Mark and Irish Mike have overtaken me. That's ok. I can live with that.

Last year, Irish Mike did 2 hours 58 minutes in Brighton without trying, then two weeks later ran the Limerick Marathon in 2 hours 55 minutes. He also has the enviable ability to finish 5th in the Dingle Marathon after demolishing half a bottle of red wine and 14 pints of Guinness the night before.

Mark, and his magnetic bracelet, ran 2 hours 49 minutes on this very course two years ago and today he's looking to go even faster. For this reason, having started a few yards behind me, something would be amiss if he hadn't gone past me by now.

Mark is the most organised person I know. Amongst other nutty events he's put together, in 2009 he planned a logistical nightmare of a relay through a string of seven countries over two weeks - a fabulous trip, beginning in Stavanger on the west coast of Norway and finishing up at a garden party on the outskirts of Brighton. There were 19 of us in all, some running the first week, some the second and a few hardcore the whole fortnight.

Up until the day before my flight to Stavanger, it was touch and go whether I would be able to make the trip. I had been ill with a gastro bug the whole of the preceding week, which entailed an extensive amount of liquidised food exiting my body from both ends. Luckily, I was over it just in time for my scheduled departure. With an agenda of knocking out around 10 miles a day for seven days, all I then had to worry about was my twisted ankle.

Six weeks earlier, five miles into a 10-mile training run and striding out on a downhill stretch, I made the schoolboy error of continuing to leg it down said hill whilst my left foot had firmly lodged itself in a rabbit hole. I subsequently limped five miles back across the Downs to where I had parked up at the top of Ditchling Beacon. I got some ice from an ice cream van, which I compressed against my now purple balloon of an ankle. It was all a bit too late. I climbed into my Landrover, fearing the heavy clutch pedal beneath my left foot. The drive home was far more torturous than any leg-press session in the gym.

The following day, with my left ankle twice the diameter of my right, I decided to cart myself off to A&E to check for any breakage. Naively, I had anticipated this would take no more than an hour. Wrong! Although there had been no fracture, there was a far more serious consequence - the procedure had taken so long that it ate into my entire evening, which meant missing out on what I was supposed to be doing, attending a gig by the Brighton-based band, The Levellers.

So, owing to illness and injury, when the day came for us to fly out to Stavanger, I had done no training for a month-and-a-half. Not to worry, accompanied by the sturdy ankle brace that Nick had flogged me, off I headed to Norway with confidence and excitement.

The event had been badged 'NorBel', deriving its name from the course that would take us from Norway to Belgium. Between us, including the home straight from Dover to Brighton, we would chalk up a grand total of 1312 miles. On all accounts, by electing to run just the first week, it seems I was out there for the most scenic half of the fortnight. The entire trip took us from Norway through Sweden, Denmark, Germany, Holland and Belgium, before finishing with the final leg on home soil. This was quite a step up in Mark's organisational skills, with the 'La Fraine' adventure of two years earlier only taking in France and Spain.

There had been a two year gap between La Fraine and NorBel because that is how long it took to plan NorBel, and Mark's attention to detail would leave no stone unturned. What started out as a rough line on a map progressed over the months into spreadsheet after spreadsheet of satellite navigation points, every participant's minute-per-mile pace, costings for accommodation, costings for fuel, costings for tolls, who would be travelling in which vehicle, who would be driving each vehicle whilst the vehicle's owner was running, estimated time of arrival (to the nearest second) at every hotel and campsite, and how many chips we would each require with our evening meal. Unfortunately,

I was never able to find a suitable evening class to teach me how to decipher these spreadsheets.

Of course, getting to the stage of producing spreadsheets did not simply entail studying a map and making a couple of phone calls. Leaving nothing to chance, Mark, aided by Tom and Cathy, felt it prudent to drive the entire 1312 miles in reverse well ahead of the event - not actually driving in reverse, you understand - I mean they drove the whole course the opposite way to that which we'd be running. I think this was to enable them to check for any twigs and other such potential trip hazards that might have been lying in the road. Mark is very safety conscious.

Mark, Boycey and Malcolm were the first to arrive in Stavanger on the eve of the relay. Boycey is predominantly a very fast 800m runner... but has also smashed 3 hours for a marathon. Malcolm, if ever he could be bothered to commit to some training, would be a fantastic runner. Unfortunately, he can't be bothered!

Donned in our matching luminous yellow tee-shirts, on the evening of our arrival we all ran a short leg of a mile or so in order to get ahead of the game. For most of us there had been a degree of stiffening up on the flight over, so a 10 to 15 minute jog helped us loosen up a little ahead of our longer stints in the days ahead. It was good to get the first part of our course out of the way. It involved some busy road sections on which the accompanying vehicles would have to make frequent stops to facilitate a regular changeover of runners. From a 'Safety First' point of view, it soon became clear that our priority that first evening was to keep Malcolm securely locked away in the back of Mark's campervan. Having worked his way through his fortnight's supply of beer on the 20-hour drive from the UK, now drowning out the radio with a style of singing somewhat akin to the early rounds of The X Factor, Malcolm was not quite able to disguise the fact that he was off his face.

On return to our campsite, the compact and bijou log cabin, which would sleep me and three others that night, was converted this evening into a dining room for 14. We had been joined by Mark's Norwegian friends. What wonderful people – they had prepared a fantastic meal for us all, cooked at their house and brought to our campsite for demolishing. And to complement such exquisite cuisine, we each cracked into our respective stashes of beer, which had been carefully loaded onto the various vehicles a week earlier. Having researched the price of alcohol in these parts, this was considered by Mark to be the most important matter for inclusion in his pre-event planning. In fact, when he originally designed the conversion of his newly acquired van into a camper, to give priority to the accommodation of a suitably large fridge in order to pander to his drinking hobby, he was quite insistent that he would be willing to do away with more secondary accessories such as stove, lavatory and steering wheel.

There should have been 15 of us dining together rather than just the 14 who were squeezed into my cabin. This is where we began to be marvel at Satnav Steve's expertise in the functionality of a satellite navigation system.

I had not previously met Satnav Steve. As I understand it, prior to the NorBel trip he was just called Steve. On each of the 14 evenings that followed, as the rest of us tucked into supper, Satnav Steve would immerse himself for an hour or so in spreadsheets, map and satellite navigation system. Taking into account the next day's distances that each of us were now feeling able to run, bearing in mind our various injury updates, Satnav Steve would calculate the exact coordinates to the nearest millimetre of each of our revised changeover points.

And each day, when the afternoon group of runners had driven for several hours to catch the morning group of runners, to everyone's delight, down some twisty turny, Scandinavian country lane miles from civilisation, the vehicle carrying the morning runners would appear out of nowhere just as Jane, the choice voice of satnav, uttered "You have reached your destination". And there was just enough time for the ensuing runner to get out of the car and collect the baton from the incoming runner!

Considering the early start to which half the group would be subjected on the morning of our first full day, we stayed up far later than was our intention. We looked at our watches. It was still daylight outside - but it was after midnight!

By the following morning, it had become apparent that Mark's planning had not been as thorough as we had all previously given him credit for. There was a critical omission in the organisation of the sleeping arrangements. Gary and snoring room-mates, it would transpire, do not in fact go together like apple crumble and custard.

If Gary didn't get a good night's kip, it was best we all gave him a wide berth the next day. Of course, at some of the places where we stayed, if there were rooms for four people, we could just about scrape together three roomies who might be considered by the hard-of-hearing as non-snorers. Unfortunately for Gary, there were nights when a large number of us were required to sleep in relative proximity, such that any attempts to resolve this mammoth problem presented a near impossible task. And to be fair, having run the South Downs marathon just a few days before our trip, he probably needed a good rest a lot more than everyone else in the group. His only alternative options were the kitchen floor or the bath.

For those unfortunate to be on the morning shift, this necessitated setting the alarm for stupid o'clock, shovelling down some breakfast with eyes half closed, packing up all belongings to throw in the appropriate vehicle and driving to the point where the previous day's last runner had completed his or her leg. Off the first runner would go, with typically three others then driving on ahead a few miles down the road. A logical place to pull over would be at any junction where the runner would need to make a turn. There, the support crew would hang out, ready with drink, food, plasters and anything else that might be required by whoever was currently out on the road.

Personally, I was lucky with the weather. It remained dry for every one of my runs. For others (Gary), the gods were not on their side. On more than one occasion, as Gary stepped out of the van to take over the baton, the heavens opened. Ten miles later, as he handed over the baton and climbed out of his drenched clothes, the sun came out. It was quite funny really.

The scenery varied immensely. Inevitably, there were sections of our route that took us through or close to chaotic city centres. Navigating our way through one particularly busy intersection on the outskirts of Copenhagen, the support crew lost the person out running (Gary) as he followed the underpass. Even with Mark's meticulous planning, there was no way the supporting vehicle could stay close to the runner in situations such as this. I am pleased to say we eventually spotted Gary popping up from underground and we were reunited. Fortunately, stressful moments like this were relatively few.

For me, out there for just week one, I slowly weaved my way through Norway, Sweden and Denmark before finishing up on a night out on the town in Copenhagen with Boycey. I would not be participating in the Germany-Holland-Belgium half of NorBel. I chose well. The stunning mountain scenery of the northern half of the journey was just amazing. Under clear blue skies and in glorious sunshine, my lungs were filled with fresh pure mountain air. The views around every bend were simply breathtaking. With a sprained ankle far from my mind, I eased my way around the erotic curves of the road, gently undulating and with pure white powder snow to either side. Over every brow, the spectacular changing picture in front and all around me kept me mesmerised as if on some hallucinogenic drug as I cruised along with a permanent grin from ear to ear. This was the quintessence of running. Thank you, Mark.

The week passed by far too quickly and, before I knew it, I was back at home in Brighton. However, my relay participation was not quite through. It had been agreed that we would each do a stint on the Dover-to-Brighton home straight. So, seven days later, once more I set my alarm for stupid o'clock and a group of us set off on an early-morning drive down to Dover. I was to run the day's third leg.

Having spent a week meandering through three separate countries, repeatedly checking in and out of different accommodation, room sharing with a new mix of mates every night, unpacking, re-packing, changing currency, remembering to drive on the wrong side of the road, etc, etc, this final piece of the journey within a couple of hours of home would be a breeze. Well, not quite. I got lost - on my run, that is.

I found myself running along a track that gradually began to look less like a track as I proceeded through a field. And the grass in this field became progressively longer. In fact it was when the grass had reached eye-level, and I was struggling to peer over the top of it to fathom out where I was going, that I began to wonder if I had taken a wrong turning. With a river a few feet to my right and a long fence immediately in front of me stretching as far as the eye could see, my only option was to turn around and re-trace my steps half a mile back to the last turn-off that would take me over a small bridge to the other side of the river.

Getting lost was just a minor problem. What concerned me to a far greater extent was the rash which now smothered my body from head to toe and, with it, a most unbearable itch. A numbing sensation was developing in the back of my throat and my breathing was becoming laboured. I managed to get myself back on the right track and eventually found my way to the next changeover point. Cathy saw the state I was in and immediately phoned NHS Direct, who advised that I should get to a hospital as soon as possible.

We set off in Tom and Cathy's campervan in the direction of home, with the intention of turning off a few miles down the road to the nearest hospital. However, I am pleased to say that medical attention was not required. I suddenly became somewhat embarrassed by all the fuss as my symptoms eased soon after taking an antihistamine. My feeling of panic subsided and I decided that it would be far more sensible to get back home so we could get ready to go to the party that had been laid on for us all by some friends of Mark.

I'm not sure what exactly I had brushed against in that field but, whatever it was, I had very quickly developed a severe reaction to it. I actually spent several more hours in some discomfort, resting up at home, and finally making it to the party late in the afternoon. And what a fantastic party it was, as the sun continued to shine and we worked our way through the banquet that lay before us. We had all enjoyed a wonderful trip and now it was time to celebrate and reflect on our adventure.

The last 14 days had become a blur, a melange of all the highs and lows that come with running, although it was the high points that took centre stage in my memory of our journey. For me, the highlights were not just the actual running across a beautiful landscape, but all the bits in between. Taking pride of place in my memory of the trip was Mark's determined efforts at trying to communicate in Thai with the staff in a Thai restaurant in Sweden. He had started on his beer several hours earlier. Then a few more hours later, Boycey and I had to stand either side of Mark at a night club bar, so as to prop him up to prevent him falling flat on his face as complete and utter drivel dribbled out of his mouth. Priceless!

Chapter 5
"Blind Runner Coming Through!"

The pleasure of cruising along on an open road over the spectacular mountains in Norway was in sharp contrast with the densely populated marathon course in Berlin, where I now find myself.

I'm jammed in and my desire for a little personal space is totally quashed by everyone around me. The road is wide but full to capacity. It's ok though, I'm five miles in and comfortably inside 3 hour pace. The first water station comes into view. Damn it. I forgot to practise drinking water - from a plastic cup, that is. I know how to drink water from a plastic cup while standing still. I also know how to drink from a plastic bottle whilst running. Drinking water from a plastic cup whilst running, however, is as straightforward as eating pasta through a straw. I'll grab two cups on the grounds that most of the water will be spilt or inhaled through my nostrils.

The water station is on the right side of the road so, of course, every Tom, Dick and Helga veers over, en masse, to the right. It's chaos. It's like fighting to get to the bar in a busy pub on a Friday night. I need to maintain the bear-hug posture for a little while longer. Damn it. I've trodden on someone's heel. He blurts out something in German in a rather aggressive tone. I don't understand a word, but I imagine he's saying something along the lines of: "My shoe's come off, it's about to get crushed by a stampede of runners and I'm going to kill you." I can empathise with his distress. Had the tables been turned, I think I would have killed him!* I grab two cups of water. Half of the water is immediately jolted out of the cups as someone

**In case anyone thinks I should be immediately referred to a psychotherapist, I should point out that "I would have killed him" is just a turn of phrase. I have never actually had murderous intent! I cannot comment as to whether he would have actually killed me as he never caught me up.*

bumps into me, a quarter of it is snorted up my nostrils and I am quite pleased to drink the balance. It's a hot day so, ideally, I would prefer to have swallowed a little more.

I begin to wonder whether I should, in fact, have started a bit faster to get ahead of the masses. Surely it can't be this crowded a bit further up field. I bet Haile and Paula aren't this squashed in.

I am fortunate to be able to boast that, in the 2009 London Marathon, I ran for a fair while in front of all 35,000 odd participants. I was even ahead of the elite Kenyans and Ethiopians until I was overtaken just passed mile seven. Not bad considering I was just coming back from a long injury lay-off. As I may have already mentioned, I have been unable, after several attempts, to break 3 hours, so perhaps I ought to offer an explanation as to how I came to be ahead of some of the world's best marathoners, including the late Sammy Wanjiru who would go on to win with a new course record of 2:05:10.

Brighton & Hove Athletics Club had been asked to provide volunteers to help out at the start, working on one of the baggage trucks and in the information tent. Having competed in the London Marathon six times, I am familiar with the need to get up at the crack of dawn so as to get up to London well before the start. On this particular occasion, though, as staff we were required to get up before the crack of dawn. In fact, the first few hours of the day whizzed by quite quickly. Missing out on being able to run, owing to injury, I actually enjoyed the morning far more than I had anticipated. It was fun to still be involved with the event and to enjoy it from a rather different perspective.

I was part of a team whose responsibility it was to load some 1500 bags on to one of the baggage trucks. With a race start time of 9:45am, the first competitor handed in his bag around an hour before. Each runner is given a bag with a large sticker displaying their running number. Our brief was to arrange the bags as best we could into some sort of numerical order. After the start of the race, another team would take over from us as the trucks were driven to the Mall just beyond the finish line. That team would have well over two hours to sort the mess we had left for them. We had done our best but as the majority of the 1500 had held on to their bags until as close as possible to 9:45am, we suddenly found ourselves with a constant stream of bags being lobbed at us, rather than handed to us one by one, at a much faster rate than we were able to place them down in any kind of sensible order on the truck floor.

By the time the starting gun was sounded, our job was done. A couple of my baggage-handling mates and I proceeded to set about our Sunday morning training run. This would consist of a disjointed jog around London, interspersed with the odd ride on the Underground, to get to various pre-arranged points on the course to shout words of abuse / encouragement to several of our friends who were taking part in the marathon.

This was easier said than done. The course was lined with supporters several rows deep and many sections of pavement were impassable. We were trying to get to a particularly good vantage point in the vicinity of mile nine, ahead of the first of our friends who were running, as it would be possible to then dash down a couple of side streets to see them again a few minutes later. There was no way we were going to make it. Well, actually, there was one way, but it was debatable whether we would get away with it. The entire course was cordoned off both sides of the road such that no one other than those in the race was allowed on the road. But we were staff! And to prove it, we were wearing matching fluorescent yellow tops with 'STAFF' in bold letters on the front. We squeezed through the crowds who were pressed up against the barriers that lined the route and, with no-one batting an eyelid, we were soon striding out down the middle of the road past dense crowds of supporters.

As the three of us made our way around the next bend in the road, we were greeted by rapturous applause from the excited masses, their cameras at the ready. "Here they come!" I suddenly felt a wave of guilt. We smiled, gave a brief wave, and carried on. Our glory run was then brought to an abrupt halt as we pulled over to allow the real leaders to breeze past us like a train.

I can't remember which of my multitude of injuries it was that prevented me from competing in 2009; there have been so many since I took up running 15 years ago.

There was the occasion of my debut snowboarding trip. Inside the first hour of my first day on the piste, I fell awkwardly and landed on my ribs (with hipflask in breast pocket). Through the weeks that followed, it hurt to breathe deeply which, of course, meant abstaining from running, and I struggled to sleep at night. Everyone in my company was banned from telling jokes as even laughing was painful. It transpired that I had strained my intercostal muscles. The fall had happened in the February, with several weeks of marathon training in the bag in preparation for London in the April. By the time I had recovered and was able to test out my ribs on a gentle comeback jog, the marathon was just days away. I was fixed but unfit. No marathon for me!

Then there was the time I had hobbled off the sand following a game of beach volleyball. Under the impression that I had done nothing more than strain my lower calf, I continued to run, cycle and wakeboard, but the discomfort would not subside. I even went on an activity holiday a couple of months later, which involved lots of sailing and tennis. Every morning I would get up for a gentle jog to start the day, but there was nothing easy about those runs. The pain was always worse as I first stepped out of bed. Although it would ease slightly once

I'd moved around a bit, I couldn't seem to get my runs much faster than walking pace.

I eventually decided to get it checked out, so booked in to see Nick. He scanned it and diagnosed a 9mm tear in my Achilles tendon. I know exactly what had caused it. I had arrived a bit late for my scheduled game of volleyball. It had been a cold day and I hadn't allowed myself sufficient time for a warm-up. Having knocked out a series of hill reps the previous evening, I had turned up for volleyball with rather tight calf muscles - the perfect conditions for tearing one's Achilles (cold day, tight calves, no warm-up and lots of erratic bounding around on sand). Nick advised no running, cycling, tennis, etc, etc, etc for at least three months. As I left his surgery, his parting comment "Oh, and Mike, the wakeboarding ... drive the boat!" served to reinforce the point that he really didn't want me participating in any sport more active than chess. By the time I was eventually able to run again, nine months had passed.

And it seems it's not just sport that has a tendency to get me injured and stop me running. The day after booking a skiing weekend, I discovered a large lump that I suspected was a hernia. I went to see my doctor to get it checked out. It was a hernia! I wasn't clear exactly how it had happened as there were a couple of potential causes. A few days prior to my spotting what appeared to be a golf ball trying to break free, I had been twisting awkwardly in a most uncomfortable position beneath my Landrover to replace the exhaust pipe. I had also ripped out an old built-in wardrobe and I recall the doors swinging open as I carried it downstairs. In both instances, I think I was more absorbed in getting the job done rather than focusing on stabilising my core muscles as my body was jarred into twist. Anyway, nine days after seeing my doctor I was under the knife. A week later in Chamonix, I would join my friends for rides up the mountainside in a cable car, only to remain in it all the way back down as I watched them from above playing in the snow. So that was another month of no running!

D.I.Y. definitely doesn't aid my cause. When I set about digging a trench in my back garden in order to accommodate a row of bamboo trees, I hadn't anticipated falling in it and smacking my leg against a wooden plank on the way in. Fortunately, the outcome of that little incident was no more than a bloody and bruised shin, although it put me out of the Hove Prom 10k race the next morning.

I had only competed in the Hove Prom 10k once before, the previous year in fact, but hadn't raced it. Having been on my way back to fitness after some injury or other, it was yet another of those events where my sole objective was to reach the finish line. However, a week earlier it had come to light that there was a blind runner who needed a guide to accompany him around the course, as his usual guide was unable to make it. He was hoping to complete the course in about 42 minutes. Crikey, 42 minutes, blind? There must have been a mistake? Partially sighted maybe? No, definitely blind, couldn't see a thing! I was impressed.

Figuring I was in shape to run about 40 to 41 minutes, I agreed to guide him. I chatted with Keith on the phone the following day and he talked me through what I would need to do. We arranged a meeting point close to the start where a friend would drop him off, and allowed plenty of time for a warm-up and for me to get used to running with him. We were linked together with a short strap connecting my right wrist with his left. I was amazed at how relaxed Keith was, effectively putting his safety in the hands of a complete stranger.

Keith was born with congenital glaucoma. Having had a degree of sight in his early years, he lost the sight in his right eye at the age of six. The sight in his left eye gradually deteriorated and, following an unsuccessful operation at the age of 17, he eventually became totally blind by 19. I pondered over which I thought might be worse, being blind from birth or becoming blind. I couldn't begin to comprehend what Keith must have gone through, having to adapt, as an adult, to losing his sight. Keith just gets on with it.

We set off on our warm-up jog and I think I was more nervous than he was. As he knew the seafront from his younger days, I was able to describe the various landmarks we would pass and he could relate to exactly where we were. I was astonished by how confidently he strode out, and this was just our warm-up. I very quickly realized that Keith was going to be putting me through my paces that morning.

There was a large turn-out for the race and I was keen to try to avoid getting too close to the surrounding runners. We were permitted to start outside of the main pen, a few metres to the right of the masses, in relative proximity to the railings alongside the edge of the promenade. This way we avoided getting caught up in the stampede, so one less thing for me to worry about - not for long though as the course would narrow and follow the pavement.

I had been unsure about 'etiquette', never previously having run with a blind runner, but it was one of the things we had discussed over the phone, and Keith was more than happy for me to shout "Blind runner coming through!" I just hadn't imagined there would be a need to shout those words quite so often, but as Keith picked up the pace I began to wonder who was guiding whom!

It also became evident that, ideally, to guide a blind runner over 10 km, the guide really ought to be able to run the course several minutes faster. There were two factors that would cause me to slow down, which I hadn't quite appreciated. Firstly, there was my inability to swing my right arm as freely as usual. And secondly, for one who is normally unable to offer much more than a grunt when anybody tries to open up a conversation mid-race, having to effectively provide a running commentary for the entire 10 km I was completely knackered well before half way.

He towed me around in 42 minutes 38 seconds. I just hope I hadn't held him back too much.

Keith has since gone on to demonstrate his talent by twice winning the 'Assisted Race' category in the Great North Run. In the most recent one, permitted to set off ahead of the masses, he ran for three quarters of the route with his guide running alongside, but unattached. Only when caught by the elite runners did they join up with a wrist-to-wrist strap in order to avoid the risk of any collision. As he now reflects on that run, he describes with excitement the immense freedom he experienced being able to run untethered, an emotion the majority of us will never quite comprehend.

And remarkably, having almost drowned as a child, Keith has also overcome a fear of swimming to compete in triathlons up to half-ironman distance. Respect!

I have utmost admiration for anyone able to compete in multi-discipline events as I find one activity troublesome enough. I was fortunate enough to meet Britain's number-one heptathlete, Jess Ennis, last year. She was doing some promotional work at the Women's 5k Challenge in Hyde Park. I just happened to be there because Tom and I were supporting Cathy and Fiona.

Having spotted her, I promptly texted Mark who has, let's say, a bit of a soft spot for Jess. His reply was "Tell Jess I love her!"... So, I did! As an ice-breaker I used the fact that Mark had, the day before, been the first Brit in a 50-mile race in Dingle, South-West Ireland. She smiled at me in a bemused fashion, kindly signed her autograph for Mark and, I imagine, was then quite pleased to turn her attention to the next person in the queue.

Over the last 15 years, I have come to realize that getting injured and working my way back from injury is as central to my sport as owning a pair of training shoes. Of course, cynics who would rather stay indoors and watch TV, will no doubt grin smugly and say, "I told you that running is bad for you!" and continue to question in bewilderment, "So, why do you run?"

As mentioned earlier, the many injuries that have led to enforced periods of abstinence from running have not necessarily been caused by running. Gardening, volleyball, D.I.Y. and snowboarding have all played their part in temporarily putting me out of action, yet I am not deterred, and I am not about to take on the sedentary lifestyle of a couch potato. To abstain from physical activity and not to push myself now and then to discover the extent of my body's capability would drive me insane. And I must be doing something right - I completed my most recent marathon, last year in Brighton at the age of 44, five minutes faster than my debut marathon in London at the age of 30.

When I set about training for that first marathon at the tail end of 1996, prior to which I had not embarked on much more than the occasional jog, little did I know how addictive my new sport would become.

I was 17 years of age when I first considered running a marathon, albeit it was a relatively short-lived idea at the time. I spent my school years in Wolverhampton which, in 1984, was to host its third marathon. I knew nothing about marathon running back then. In fact I had run no more than a couple of miles when this bizarre idea came into my head. The best I had mustered in my schoolday athletics was a 1500 metres race on sports day in an uninspiring 5 minutes 47 seconds. I showed absolutely no potential as an athlete. However, there was something exciting about the prospect of taking part in what I perceived to be the ultimate test of endurance. I set about doing some training – well, not proper training. I didn't have a structured programme to follow. There was no coach, no specific 'V0$_2$ max' sessions, no 'lactic threshold' runs, no hill reps, no 'strength and conditioning' work-outs. In fact, all my training consisted of was going for a few runs a week, all at more or less the same pace. Three weeks went by and I had reached a level where I could keep going, without stopping, for six miles. Unfortunately, this is where I gave up. I had not even reached a quarter of the required distance. My newfound sport had been taking up too much of my time. I had exams to think about. Running could wait.

Through the decade that followed, there were a couple of further half-hearted attempts to set about some regular running with a view to building up to marathon distance. Unfortunately, on each occasion I found myself repeating the process of preparing for Wolverhampton, getting my longest run up to around six miles and then finding some reason to take my goal no further.

As I look back on those days, I struggle to comprehend why it was that I found it seemingly impossible to progress beyond the initial stages of marathon preparation. I never picked up injuries back then, so it's not as though I was forced to stop due to calf strains, twisted ankles, torn Achilles or any other such niggle that now hinders my cause. Nor did I lack ambition.

So why, on several occasions, did I set myself this bizarre running goal, yet not have the desire to follow it through to completion?

I think the reason was that I lacked focus, and the reason I lacked focus was because I didn't *know* marathon running. I had no experience of it and there were no reference points. I had never met anyone who had done it. I had seen no films or documentaries and had read no books about it. In short, I had no idea what it was that I would be spending several months training towards. Times meant nothing to me - I had no comprehension of what was deemed fast, slow or average and I certainly couldn't guess within an hour what the world record was. Because of this, I had no target finish time and, without one, I guess the simple objective of just completing the course was not enough for me.

Several years on, and a seasoned marathoner, I am addicted.

When asked why I run, I find it hard to provide a short, concise answer. I run because I love running. I get immense satisfaction from challenging myself, from pushing myself through the pain barrier and from the excitement of wondering what pleasure awaits on the other side. Only when you have been there is it possible to understand the intensity of emotion induced by the roar of the supporting crowds just as you think you are depleted of energy and your legs are beginning to buckle. The thrill of overtaking a rival in the home straight of a race, or beating someone for the first time after numerous head-to-head battles, can only be understood once experienced. And most of all, the rush of achieving personal best times is, for me, the icing on the cake. Every day, very gradually, our bodies slowly wear out; our muscles tire and weaken over time, joints deteriorate and our organs function less efficiently than they did in our youth. By definition, achieving PBs is a defiance of the ageing process - getting older, but faster!

Particularly gratifying is that these various glorious moments of pleasure are felt so intensely because they follow long periods of pain and discomfort. Only when you have raced and pushed yourself to your limits will the concept of running being a drug bear any significance. The effects are often short-lived, in my personal experience the buzz lasting no more than one week, at its briefest just a few seconds, and this sometimes after a lead-in period of several months or more. But, with such an intense rush, it is definitely worth it - I think this is why I run!

As recently as last year, after 14 years of regular running, I knocked out a PB for 800m in a time of 2 minutes 20 seconds, and I am still confident that there are more PBs to come. My quest for PBs is clearly helped by the fact that I only took up running properly at the age of 30. Had I been racing since my teens, I would no doubt have reached my peak at some point in my twenties. However, I am under no illusion that my getting progressively faster will continue indefinitely. So far, I have continually managed to discover improved training techniques, learned how to manage and prevent injuries, become more informed about fuel intake, and found numerous small ways to fine-tune my performance on race day.

I am not perturbed though that this trend cannot continue forever. One of the great things about the sport of running and the ageing process is that in the majority of races there are age categories. This means I can compare my performances with competitors of a similar age to myself rather than those 25 years younger. This is where I benefit from having taken up running relatively late in life. When I began 15 years ago, I would finish most races a fair way down the field and be compared with everyone else taking part as I was still in the 'senior' category, albeit at the upper end of it, rather than in any of the veteran categories. Whilst I have slowly improved over the years, and am now a 'vet', I have noticed that many of my original rivals, who started running much earlier, have gradually slowed down or dropped out with injury, such that I now tend to rank much higher as a vet than I ever did in the senior category.

In recent years, in the same vein as age categories, we have seen the introduction of age-graded performance. One's age-grading for any given distance is determined by the world record time for a person of the same age and sex. This, of course, provides a great source of banter with running mates who might beat you by a narrow margin but score a lesser age-grading owing to the fact that they are a year younger. In such scenarios, the age-grading system is of huge importance! I have recently managed to exceed an age-grading of 80% for my performance in a couple of short-distance races. Over marathon distance, however, I have not come close. In fact, this highlights the bewilderment of the majority of my running circle as to why on earth I persist with marathon running when I clearly have far more competence over shorter distances. Conversion tables exist to provide a realistic expectation of finish times for any given distance based upon performance over other distances. My PBs for 800m, 1 mile, 3000m, 5 km and 10 km would suggest that I should be smashing 3 hours for a marathon. My half-marathon PB would suggest I could just about sneak in under 3 hours.

I am pleased to have run a mile in 4 minutes 55 seconds. Several of my mates who have broken 3 hours for a marathon have not got close to 5 minutes for a mile. Without a doubt, I should have ditched marathon running years ago. Unfortunately, though, I can't. I'm not exactly sure what it is that keeps my determination alive. I would be inexplicably ecstatic if I were to cross the line in 2:59:59, yet utterly depressed if ever I finished in 3:00:00.

How can one solitary second be of such profound importance?!

But, it is! It most definitely is! It's the difference between failure and success. For a huge chunk of my life I have failed, yet I'm not a failure. There is something special and unique about clocking a time which begins with a '2'. It would be a light-year leap into a club frequented by every elite marathoner who ever lived. Not only would I be able to join my mates who have already made it into the sub-3 club, and no longer feel like an outsider, but I would be in the same category as the current world record holders, Haile and Paula, who are now no doubt a fair way down the road in front of me and totally oblivious and indifferent to the fact that their club is about to be joined by a new member.

Chapter 6

'The' Marathon

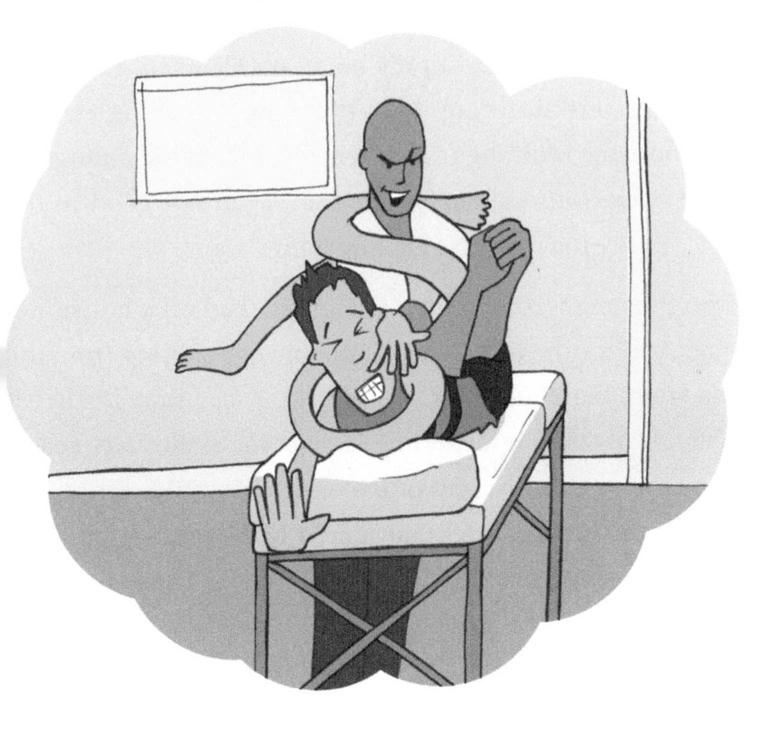

I find it easier to remain in control of the full distance if I break it down into bite-size chunks. Intervals of 5 km provide a good benchmark. The stretch between 10 km and 15 km pass with neither incident nor drama and I am reassured to note that I am cruising at an even pace, comfortably on course for under 3 hours.

I grab a plastic cup at the third drink station and share the contents between my mouth, chin and vest. The morning is getting noticeably hotter and I begin to feel the effects over the next couple of miles. It's a hot day in Berlin.

Whenever possible, I veer to the side of the road where there is a little shade, but it's not easy. There are too many other runners all trying to do the same and along most of the route the buildings on either side are not tall enough to protect us from the sun's harsh rays. I'm not good in the heat. I pray that it won't get any hotter.

Don't get me wrong, I love going for a run on a hot sunny day. And for the thousands of people applauding from the roadside, the conditions are perfect. I fear though that it will take its toll on me in the second half of the race. I can't afford to become dehydrated as that would cause my muscles to cramp. And that would be like riding my bike with the brakes on. I know what it's like to run with cramp. I know all too well!

It's ok, though, I glance at my Garmin as I go through mile 12 - I'm on course for sub-3. Not quite moving at my planned pace owing to a slight hindrance by the masses all around me and the loss of a few seconds at each water station, but I'm confident I've built in sufficient margin to accommodate the small loss of time.

I pass through the half-way mark in 1:29:42. I'd planned on going through in 1:28:05, but not to worry - I have conserved some energy by running the first half a little slower than anticipated. I do my best to block out any thoughts of being zapped by the heat. I feel strong, no signs of tiring!

More importantly, I have not been overtaken by anyone in fancy dress. When I ran my first London Marathon I was most appreciative of the constant shouts of encouragement, although a tad bemused as to why so many supporters along the route were shouting "Come on Tiger!" It later came to light that it wasn't actually me at whom the shouts were aimed, but the runner behind who was dressed in a tiger suit. The moment he overtook me at about mile 23, giving the crowd a wave as he bounded past me, I should have known that the London Marathon and I were not destined for each other. At least, unlike Simon*, I have never been overtaken by a toilet! (I should clarify, this was not an actual toilet but a runner dressed as one.)

So many people refer to the London Marathon as 'The' Marathon as if it were the only one in the world. And in fact I too was guilty of the same, not appreciating in my early running days that there are hundreds of marathons staged throughout the year all over the world.

**Simon is yet to break 3 hours. However, I am reasonably confident that he would have smashed it long ago... if only he could be bothered to train on days when it rains.*

Having said that, there is something special about the London Marathon, certainly the most high profile annual event on the athletics calendar in the UK, attracting around 120,000 hopefuls from across the globe, all vying for a place. It raises millions of pounds for charities, attracts world class runners owing to the flat and fast nature of the course and weaves its way around some of the most famous landmarks in the country. Each year, numerous celebrities take part and, with a route lined with live musical entertainment and barbecues in pub gardens, it provides for a fantastic day out for spectators.

If I were going to run a PB, it had to be in London - not any low profile marathon that no-one knew was taking place. So, that's why I selected London for my debut marathon ... and my second, third, fourth, fifth and sixth.

Moving to Brighton in the summer of 1996 and joining the athletics club in the November, I found myself slotting in with a large group of runners all in the early stages of training for London the following April. This was my first proper introduction to running, and certainly the first time I had run with a group. I had made a passing comment to a colleague at work that I quite fancied running 'The Marathon' and his response was that I should seek out someone named Sam at the Jog Shop. My colleague had just popped in there the previous week for a pair of training shoes and had come away with the distinct impression that its owner, Sam, was the hub of 'all things running' in Brighton.

Off I went that weekend to find Sam. And it transpired that he was, indeed, a most useful contact in my quest to find out more about marathon running, having completed one himself in 2 hours 18 minutes!

I explained that I had recently been doing three runs a week, my furthest being from Grand Avenue to the marina and back - about six miles. He suggested I join his training group, which met at 7:30pm every Tuesday on the track at Withdean Stadium, temporary home of Brighton and Hove Albion Football Club. In the early days, several of those Tuesday evenings were spent in nearby Withdean Park whilst repairs were carried out to the dated track that was beginning to resemble a patchwork quilt. In fact, 15 years on, it still does!

The Tuesday sessions were designed to improve speed by carrying out various permutations of reps in the range of 200m to 1 km (always totalling 6 km) and always finishing up with a mile. Well, almost a mile - four laps to be precise, so 1600 metres. (A mile is 1609 metres.) I hadn't quite comprehended the fact that all the reps that made up those sessions were supposed to be run at even effort, and consequently the mile became the focus every week. I would treat the mile as a race and, as such, I never got the best out of those training sessions. I did, however, dramatically reduce my mile time. On two occasions in 1999 I broke five minutes, knocking out a couple of 4:55s, which I figured fared well compared with the 5:47 for 1500m in my teens.

At 9 o'clock every Sunday morning, the group would meet by the Peace Statue on Hove Lawns. We would head out eastwards alongside the beach and clifftop before turning inland at Telscombe Tye. From there, we would meander through the picturesque countryside of the South Downs, every couple of weeks extending the course by a mile or two.

Year after year, the bulk of my marathon training was endured on these tracks. Through the long, cold winter months, 20 or 30 of us would brave the elements, week in week out, all in preparation for one spring morning, to stand up to the challenge of The Marathon. We trained in light rain, torrential rain, sleet and snow. We ran through deep puddles, deep mud, deep shit (all kinds of it - horse dung, sheep droppings, cowpats)...

One particular fond memory from those Sunday mornings was when we all watched with concern (laughed) as a new recruit in the group found himself balancing on his left leg, having hopped for several metres through an extensive area of manure, desperately trying not to put down his right foot, his shoe having become detached from his foot some way back and now well beyond reach.

We watched for a while in order to savour the moment before Steve* set about doing the gentlemanly thing, wading through said manure to retrieve the shoe.

On a similar occasion, my training partner Kader did not seem to find his sense of humour when I thought it might be a bit funny to rugby tackle him to the ground in a sea of wet mud four miles into a 22 mile run. It still tickles me a decade later when I recall jogging alongside him for the last couple of miles along a busy Brighton seafront, as he was caked in mud from head to toe.

Kader is one of the more colourful characters in my running circle, one of the first people to whom I was introduced when I joined the club. Previously a boxer, having been selected to represent Algeria in the 1980 Moscow Olympics, he has since gone on to run numerous marathons including around a dozen in under 3 hours. Endurance running being his strength, he has competed in the annual London to Brighton race (circa 55 miles) on a multitude of occasions, as well as the Comrades Marathon in South Africa (also around 55 miles) and the Marathon des Sables (155 miles in one week through the Sahara desert).

**Steve's the guy who got a mention in Chapter 1. I commented that he still needs to pull his finger out. To be fair, Steve has since discovered that he can continue all day long at the same pace, so it seems he's quite a good ultra runner. (Please refer to Glossary of Terms for 'Ultra runner'.)*

Most people on the Brighton running scene will know Kader as the brutal sports massage therapist who makes grown men cry as he digs his knuckles and elbows into tight calves, quads, hamstrings and I.T. bands. And as if leaving your battered body in a weeping mess on his couch is not enough, he will proceed to contort your body into positions that really ought to be saved for a rag doll needing to be pushed through a small letterbox. However, there must be something to be said for Kader's torture sessions as I repeatedly find myself returning for more of the same, each time emerging sore but able to run more freely.

Having stated the above, I recently attended a seminar at which the marathon legend Ron Hill explained that he has only ever had two massages, having completed 115 marathons and not having had a day off running since 1964. One of Ron's principles in life is to never leave any stone unturned. He can't have heard of Kader*!

So, on with the long Sunday training runs, through wind and precipitation, over soggy ground, loose stones, frosty fields and, as winter turns into spring, through long grass to remind myself I have hay fever! And to further enhance the character-building of these Sunday mornings, there is a nice mix of hills of varying degrees of ascent. The

**Very sadly, Kader (Abdelkader Sidi-Moussa) has died since the above was written, and is a huge loss to the running community in Sussex.*

significant sections of the course are aptly referred to by names such the North Face, the Snake and Death Valley.

Each week, through the latter stages of my trudge over the Downs and back along the sea front, I observe a pattern emerging – I begin to hallucinate as I see vivid images of myself slumped over a large Sunday roast with sprouts, carrots, parsnips, peas, boiled potatoes, roast potatoes, gravy... Breakfast was half a day ago, and all I've consumed since then is a couple of small energy gels and a bottle of water – I'm very fond of food, I'm depleted, I need to eat! Eventually, we all arrive back at the Peace Statue for a nice cup of tea and a slice of cake in the adjacent Meeting Place cafe to tide us over until lunch. I can't stick around in the cafe for too long though - I need to get back home to immerse my weary legs in a bath of cold water to give them half a chance of being able to survive the track on Tuesday.

The Tuesday and Sunday runs would represent the core training sessions each week, with lots more miles crammed into the days in between. My maximum weekly mileage, attained three to four weeks before the big day, would typically reach 50 to 60, with a couple of warm-up races thrown in along the way. Old favourites would be the Brighton Half Marathon in February and either the Hastings Half Marathon or Worthing 20 miler in March. Each year, I have emerged from these warm-up races with confidence in my ability to sneak in under 3 hours.

On the Wednesday preceding The Marathon, my running buddies and I would converge at Brighton railway station for a day trip up to London to mooch around the marathon exhibition. Here we would register for the grand occasion and collect our running numbers along with goody bags. On entry, we were welcomed by the theme music from Chariots of Fire. In my first London Marathon year, this immediately made the hairs on the back of my neck stand up. I felt a rush of adrenaline, visualising myself crossing the finish line with the first displayed digit on the overhead clock being '2'. Several years later, and on my sixth visit to the exhibition, the tune begins to grate.

We would wander up and down the aisles, checking out the numerous stands selling running kit, playing 'spot the celebrity' on our way around. Year after year, I set out on a mission to find a stall selling a suitable contraption to port my energy gels, repeatedly unsuccessful. The highlight would be thirty seconds spent on a treadmill, provided by one of the principal shoe manufacturers, for the purpose of analysing one's gait. A wave of panic would then set in as I am told that the shoes I have planned on wearing in four days' time are totally inappropriate for my running style. I then enter a new phase of deliberation until the shops close at 5:30pm on the Saturday and I no longer have a choice. I'll be sticking with the inappropriate shoes I'm used to!

Minimal running would be done in the last few days in order to rest my legs, now with hundreds of miles in them. It concerned me a little that perhaps I shouldn't have spent so much time on my feet traipsing around London on the Wednesday, but it would be ok, Kader had given my legs a good battering on the Thursday.

By the Saturday evening, well rested and with a tonne of pasta trying to fight its way out of every pore of my skin, I would retire to bed for an early night. Totally pointless! Waking up in the early hours, perspiring with nerves and excitement, there's no way I'm going to get back to sleep. It's 4:30am. There remains almost two hours before I have to make the five minute drive to Withdean Stadium where the bus is to pick us up. Having laid out my kit the night before, all there is to do between now and driving to Withdean is put on my kit and have breakfast.

Bearing in mind this is the early days of my marathoning, getting ready was a rather simple affair and didn't require more than about 15 minutes. I decide to get up and pace around.

As I arrive at the stadium, my heart begins to race as a long bus queue is already forming. These are the friends I have met over the last few months. For some, with several marathons under their belts, their experience enables them to wait calm and composed, conserving energy. For me, a first-timer, I'm like a child on Christmas morning told he can't open his presents until mid-day.

The journey up to London is slow – I've never before witnessed such a constant stream of visitors to a bus toilet. And this is just the first round! There will be a good two or three more bowel-emptying attempts before we line up at the start.

Finally, our bus reaches Blackheath. This is it! This is the big day! The crowds progressively build as thousands of us from across the UK and beyond all merge together to take part in The Marathon. Huge, brightly-coloured advertising balloons hover above the starting area and celebrities are being interviewed. Supporting friends and relatives give a last hug and excitedly offer well wishes as they part company to shout valued words of encouragement from the sidelines further down the course. Bodies are wrapped in foil to keep warm, some people are stretching, some are jogging slowly, some are sipping energy drinks, and the more experienced are lying down to conserve valuable energy stores.

Eventually, the time has come. I've dropped off my bag on the relevant baggage truck and I'm standing at the start... well, jumping up and down at the start! Having first had the idea to run a marathon at the age of 17, here I finally am, seconds away from actually doing it. Several months of training in the bag, I'm ready to embark on my first marathon, 'The' Marathon, and I have the ability to complete it in less than 3 hours.

Well, of course, I didn't do it in less than three hours... I got around in 3:08, and the next time in 3:15, then 3:02. The following year, I had the bright idea of abstaining from alcohol for two full months before the big day. What a waste of time that was! Not even a liqueur chocolate had passed my lips from mid-February to mid-April. Ok, so I got a PB by 23 seconds, but still 3:02.

2003 was a bad year. I hit the wall at mile 20 and began to walk. Although ahead of 3 hour pace, there was absolutely no way I could continue. My lower back was hurting and both hips were seizing up. I had slowed significantly in the 20th mile and was no longer able to run freely. I have never pulled out of a marathon, preferring to press on in pain rather than give up. But that particular occasion was the closest I have come to seeking out the nearest tube station and making my way home. I had to get my head to try and convince my body that it was indeed capable of soldiering on through the final 10 km.

Music being played all along the course normally has the effect of providing a lift, an adrenaline rush, an injection of energy. However, for me at that particular moment, to rub salt into my wounds, as I began to walk at mile 20, it was as though the song being played was directed straight at me. It was Coldplay's 'In My Place' with the lyrics "I was scared, tired and under-prepared"!

Ironically, the following week, I met Coldplay's Chris Martin. I had been fortunate enough to take a trip to New York for a long weekend on one of Concorde's last flights, shortly before it was retired from the skies. On arrival at JFK airport, as Simon and I waited for our bags to appear on the conveyor belt, standing next to us were Chris and his actress wife Gwyneth Paltrow. Relaxed and uninhibited owing to several glasses of champagne over the preceding four hours, I had no qualms about going up to Chris and telling my story. His initial thoughts at my opening sentence "Chris, hi, a quick story for you... last Sunday I ran in the London Marathon..." must have been along the lines of "Who is this nutter? Someone get him away!" Fortunately, I managed to hold his attention long enough for him to realise he featured in the recounting of my 20-mile moment. "What a lovely story!" he responded. I was delighted that he had spoken to me. Their baggage arrived and they made a swift exit!

Shortly after I had stopped running at mile 20, I decided that there was no way I was going to give up and pull out. I managed to jog and walk the last six miles, eventually crossing the line in 3 hours 28 minutes.

In 2005, my training had been sporadic due to an ongoing foot problem. Up until the Wednesday before the big day, it had been questionable as to whether I would be able to compete. On that Wednesday, I had to make a decision – either head up to the exhibition in London to register and collect my number, or return my entry for deferral to the following April. I decided to run. I did 3:09. Having then spent an eternity staggering and weaving beyond the finish line the short distance required to collect my bag and repatriate myself with my Brighton & Hove mates at the pre-arranged meeting point of 'tree B' on Horse Guards Parade, I promptly collapsed in a heap. I'm not sure how long I lay there motionless, but I was eventually brought back to life as Ian* prised open my jaws and shoved some sweets in.

So, I was unable to deliver on the London stage. I had a go six times in nine years, mission unaccomplished!

But now, six years on, with half a dozen Londons and a Brighton behind me, I have never felt as confident as I do today. The first half of Berlin is in the bag. I get a

**I am pleased to note that Ian has completed far more marathons than me and not got close to 3 hours. However, particular respect should be paid for the occasion when he ran a cross-country marathon racing a horse (whilst dressed as a horse).*

psychological boost in the knowledge that I'm now heading home in the direction of the Brandenburg Gate.

My legs are showing no signs of tiring. I think this is attributed to having trained on a different terrain to previous years. I took the view that the reason for everything hurting so much during the latter stages of my previous marathons was because I had only ever done minimal training on a flat road. The bulk of my long Sunday runs had historically taken place on hilly, off-road terrain, yet I was preparing for 26 miles on a flat road. I have consulted a number of experienced marathoners on this point, and the opinion is mixed. However, in the build-up to Berlin, I was acutely aware that if I were to achieve a better result, something had to change. Running out of ideas, I concluded that I should carry out the majority of my long training runs on a flat road.

It is now, as I approach the final third of Berlin, that I am feeling the benefits of having battered my legs through mile after mile of pounding up and down Brighton's sea front.

With eight miles remaining, I have no back discomfort, no tightness in my buttocks and it's looking like my hips are not going to seize up. My quads feel strong and, importantly, my calves, which are normally my weakest link, are still intact and giving me no reason to suspect that they are going to let me down.

The blob of anaesthetic gel on the ball of my right foot was most definitely a good move as I'm experiencing zero discomfort in the area that has felt bruised for the last three weeks, and I did not apply so much of the gel as to remove sensation from the rest of my foot.

And I definitely selected the correct shoes as I have not found it necessary, on this occasion, to resort to altering the position of my toes prior to each foot strike in order to prevent blister accumulation.

The volume of pasta consumed since Thursday morning would seem to have been pitched at an appropriate level, as would the timing and choice of energy gels. I know this as I go through mile 20 in 2 hours 17 minutes 26 seconds. I have so far averaged exactly 6:52 per mile, which means I'm bang on course for 3 hours. If I continue at this pace, which I know I can, for the final 10 km, I'll just need to find one solitary second to sneak in inside 3 hours and my mission will at long last be accomplished.

And I still have two caffeine-laced gels securely attached to my left wrist. Thank you, Fiona, for constructing my gel wrist band with supporting loops of optimum tension. I know I got you to re-stitch them three times, but your efforts were not in vain as perfect grippage has been attained. My Garmin is also to be applauded for doing a fine job of carrying out its secondary task of wedging the gels in place to prevent flappage.

What on earth could go wrong now - other than the possibility of a huge dog springing up out of nowhere and wiping me out, as happened to my old mate, John, three years ago at the age of 75, resulting in a couple of broken ribs and a punctured lung? I figure that would be such an unlikely occurrence, I quickly remove it from my thoughts.

With more energy in the tank and the assurance of knowing there is further glycogen to call upon, along with a couple of kicks of caffeine, I push on, quietly confident that this is going to be my day - at long last, on my eighth attempt in 15 years, I'm finally going to crack it.

Chapter 7

Tupperware Containers and Potatoes

I've competed in races over an extensive range of distances, so really a marathon is just another race. But the matter of ensuring that there is enough fuel in the tank is something that does not necessitate much consideration for races shorter than marathon distance, particularly at the shorter end of the spectrum.

In fact, I have come to realize that the sport of running, while in essence fairly simple, can actually be rather diverse. Every event has its own characteristics and training requirements. Footwear needs to be specific to the terrain and distance being covered. For certain events the course needs to be recced in advance, particularly for tricky off-road routes with an absence of marshals. Races of longer distance, such as a marathon, will predominantly use the aerobic system, whereas sprint distances are mainly anaerobic. For team events and relays, recognition of each member's strengths and weaknesses is key to overall success. And, most importantly, I have found that performance over certain distances can be enhanced by downing significant quantities of beer the night before.

I have yet to be brave enough to put away more than a pint on the eve of a marathon, risking dehydration mid-race and potentially wasting several months of training. But some of my 5k races have definitely benefited from lots of Guinness being poured down my neck. I once knocked 29 seconds off my parkrun PB having consumed six pints of Guinness the previous evening, getting to bed at 2am and waking with a hangover 30 minutes before the start. I'm not exactly sure of the science behind the improvement in speed brought about by consumption of the black stuff, but it seems to work, and I quite like it!

In terms of differing characteristics from one race to another, probably the polar opposite to the 26.2 miles of flat tarmac road, on which I now find myself, would be the national cross-country championships on Parliament Hill. I was somewhat unprepared for my first participation in that event. Prior to Parliament Hill, I had minimal experience of cross-country, the consequence being that I turned up with a totally inappropriate pair of road-running shoes. Prone to frequently picking up injuries, I figured I would benefit more from the cushioning of such shoes than the grip of spikes. How wrong I was! The 15 km of mud beneath my feet provided far more cushioning than any running shoe.

The annual national cross-country champs rotates each year between a variety of venues including Parliament Hill on Hampstead Heath, North-West London. I've never done any of the others, but I've most definitely 'done' Parliament Hill - or rather, it did me! The first 200m section of the course is all uphill. And thanks to the previous day's heavy rainfall combined with the girls' race churning up the sloping earth, their race having taken place immediately before the men's, I was completely exhausted by the time I reached the top of that first hill. My shoes had served no purpose. They were caked in wet mud inside and out and, as for grip, I may as well have worn a pair of slippers.

So, 200m done, approximately 14.8 km to go. The remainder of the course was not dissimilar to that opening hill ... except the mud got deeper! Of course, in any race that meanders left and right, the shortest route follows the inside bends. Unsurprisingly, the inside bends on Parliament Hill were the muddiest - not a blade of grass in sight! I worked out that I could run much better (or rather, less slowly) by instead taking the lesser trodden outside bends, taking a particularly wide berth of the masses. In doing so, I must have covered a considerably greater distance than everyone else, but at least my shoes remained attached to my feet.

The most memorable section of Parliament Hill was a particularly soggy dip in the ground, a good 12 inches deep and about 20 feet in diameter. Clearly, for the spectators familiar with the course, this would be the highlight of the event. Some spectators were dotted along the route, but around this deep mud pond were huddled large numbers of folk greatly entertained by all the slipping and sliding and detachment of footwear. This particular section of the course was situated snugly between a pair of gate posts, thus providing no option to skirt the perimeter of the mess that lay before me. I waded through the treacle of earth, successfully maintaining my balance and, unlike others, managed to come out the other side still on two feet. In fact, I was relieved to go on and complete the course without a fall or loss of shoe –

although, with hindsight, I think I would have got around faster barefoot.

Not only are there differing characteristics from one race to another, but there should also be a distinction between those events that are to be taken seriously as against those meant solely for fun. With the degree of fun to be had, there tends to be a directly proportionate link to the amount of alcohol consumed.

A marvellous example of beer-assisted run fun is the annual ascent and descent of the hill between the Shepherd & Dog and Devil's Dyke pubs, in celebration of Shaun* and Sara's wedding anniversary.

Of course, it was Shaun who came up with the idea for this event, pandering to his two favourite hobbies – drinking beer and running. However, I'm sure that Sara's agreement for this to proceed provides her with a strong argument to be taken out to the restaurant of her choice at Shaun's expense.

We typically arrive early at the Shepherd & Dog to share a couple of jugs of ale. Once everyone is present, the race begins. This quite simply involves downing a pint, then clambering the best part of a mile up the hillside as fast as our wobbling legs can carry us, to the Devil's Dyke where

**Shaun is considerably better than I am at both running and beer-drinking. He has a personal best marathon time of 2 hours 51 minutes.*

a couple of volunteers wait patiently with more beer so that we can swiftly sink another pint before immediately hacking it downhill back to the Shepherd & Dog. The regular beer drinkers amongst us always seem to have a marked advantage. In celebration of completing Shaun's Shandy Shuffle, the remainder of the afternoon and evening tends to be spent in the pub.

A more recent addition to the calendar of annual running events not to be taken too seriously is the Super Heroes 5k and 10k up and down Brighton sea front. This is organised by the splendid Pass It On Africa charity with the objective of raising funds to enable the construction of schools in poverty-stricken countries such as Kenya, Ghana and The Gambia. On one Sunday morning in May, the promenade is transformed into a carnival of Spider-men, Wonder Women, Incredible Hulks and Lara Crofts to name but a few. Brighton & Hove Athletics Club's own super hero Bionic Bladder Man (otherwise known as Richard) can normally be seen striding out in full and unique regalia, defying the odds by still running after recovering from a serious bout of bladder cancer.

Amongst other significant achievements, Bionic Bladder Man, in his youth, became British schoolboy cross country champion, and in more recent years has devoted a significant proportion of his spare time in a coaching and organisational role for the club. Despite his illness, he has battled on regardless, continuing to train, motivate and support other athletes, and been justly awarded the title of Sussex Coach of the Year. Bionic Bladder Man, in my view, is the linchpin of our club.

'Veules-Les-Roses' is most definitely in the 'fun' category. The quaint French village is situated 20 km to the south of Dieppe and, for several years, a group of 20 to 30 of us from Brighton took part in their annual relay event. Each May bank holiday we would group together in half a dozen cars to drive the short distance to Newhaven where we would catch the Friday morning ferry to Dieppe. With Steve and Annie Sparks, year after year performing a marvellous role of overseeing all matters organisational, their packaging of the trip became affectionately known as Sparky Tours.

Once on the ferry, the opening sequence of activities would go something like: (a) make way to bar, followed by (b) drink beer. Beer drinking would typically come to a temporary close at around 2am on the Saturday morning in a Scottish bar, which I seem to recall was called The Scottish Bar. In the intervening period, at some point on the Friday afternoon, there would be the drawn-out process of checking into a cheap Dieppe hotel as we all deliberated over who would share with whom.

Mid-morning on the Saturday, we remembered why we were there and drove to Veules-Les-Roses where the relay race would begin at noon. We were always greeted by a booming commentary over a loudspeaker by a French man sitting behind a small table set up on the pavement. His voice was so loud that, even without a tannoy, I think he would have been clearly heard in the neighbouring village.

We formed teams of three. The course was a loop of approximately four miles, with the start and finish being on the road adjacent to the loud commentator's table. The route began on the road, but within a couple of minutes we would find ourselves climbing a steep and twisting path up to the clifftop, then through fields and more off-road paths before descending back down to the village, following the picturesque streets to the finish.

Runner 'A' for each team went first, followed by 'B', then 'C'. Once 'C' had finished his or her leg, all three would re-run the course together. Whilst the French took the race quite seriously, us lot from Brighton turned up hungover from the Friday's excesses. With no specific race plan or rationale behind the formation of our teams, it was more a case of those suffering the worse hangovers being selected to run leg 'A' so as to give more recovery time before being required to stagger around the course for a second time.

In the context of the whole weekend, the race itself represented a relatively minor part of the overall proceedings, although there was one notable occasion when half of our runners got lost on the way round. This was entirely our own fault, of course, as we should have each arranged for accompaniment by a translator or, more specifically, one who could interpret the quiet French mumble of the local marshals. The climb up to the clifftop had been engulfed in thick fog and it soon became apparent to us that we were not in fact competent enough to rely on the petite chalked arrows marked in the mud to guide us around the course. On reaching the top of that first steep climb, I was faced with a decision - left or right?? I paused for a few seconds, straining to try and spot any participants ahead of me through the dense fog. In the distance to my left I could just about make out a couple of figures seemingly running away from me. I got going again, chasing after the two figures, who became three as I gradually closed the gap between them and myself.

Suddenly, as I caught them, there was a slight clearing in the mist. One of them was Steve* (whom I used to train with in Brighton until he emigrated to Dieppe to marry Francoise). We all came to an abrupt halt and, looking at each other in shock, we blurted out a series of swear words in unison. Our hearts sank as the route we had just followed came into view. We had all taken the wrong turning and were oblivious to the fact that we had been

**This is not the Steve who still needs to pull his finger out. This Steve has run a marathon in 2 hours 33 minutes.*

striding out adjacent to the clifftop with a sheer drop within a couple of metres to our left. By the time we had double-backed to the top of that first climb and re-joined the correct course, all the slower joggers now ahead of us, we had added a good five minutes to our teams' overall times.

Initially I was somewhat annoyed that the organisers had not provided adequate signage and a sufficient number of marshals, particularly as we had crossed the Channel to compete. However, I later saw the funny side... and more importantly, we were yet to enjoy the thrill of the post-race raffle which was sponsored by the local hypermarket.

Shortly after crossing the finish line with the other members of one's team, the running numbers were removed from our vests and placed in a box - those numbers now took on their secondary role as our raffle tickets. Once the last team were through the finish, we all congregated in the village hall where the Saturday evening's drinking would commence at about 3pm. To follow was a good hour of excitement as we each listened out for our number to be called... and no one was to return to Brighton disappointed. I'm not sure whether the number calling was fixed in an attempt to improve Anglo-French relations, but each and every one of us from across the water was to leave with a fantastic prize. There were bin-liners, packets of cling film and tin foil, Tupperware containers and potatoes. And to this day, ten years on, I still chuckle to myself as I recall Gary pushing his prize-winning shopping trolley through the streets of Dieppe to the ferry terminal on the Sunday morning.

The Saturday evening was spent back in Dieppe with a visit to The Scottish Bar and later on to a cheesy night club. Fortunately I wasn't spotted by a gendarme when, for some unknown reason, brimming with French wine, I took it upon myself to run naked through the Dieppe streets between pub and club.

But in terms of memorable moments from those Sparky Tours adventures across the Channel, a brief streaking down a street was to be overshadowed as another of those fabulous weekends drew to a close. Our ferry pulled out of Dieppe and we all, in sync, felt a brief wave of concern with the immediate realisation that we had left Kate behind. As we looked back to the shore, there she stood, alone, just about managing to raise a hand to wave us off. The previous night's excesses had taken their toll. As the rest of us had boarded the ferry, poor Kate had been unable to leave the bathroom to join us.

With all but one of us successfully making it back to Brighton and with no work the following day, owing to it being a bank holiday, we arranged to continue the fun in O'Neil's pub. Several hours later, greeted by rapturous applause, in walked Kate! She had survived the day's second crossing and, now in a more stable state, it was time for her to enjoy a beer!

Kate has since gone on to be the first British woman to complete a marathon in each of the globe's seven continents - and probably the first to be incontinent on all seven continents, an achievement of which I know Kate is very proud! Not accomplished in vain, having started marathon running as a way of overcoming years of depression, and having run some of the toughest marathons on earth, Kate has raised thousands of pounds for health charities worldwide.

Chapter 8

Everything's Hurting!

So, the Sparky Tours adventures were fun – no training required, no race strategy, no carbo-loading, no focus; just turn up, get lost, pick up something for the kitchen, take your clothes off in public and leave a sick friend behind at the ferry terminal. Great! Berlin? A bit different! In fact, it's fair to say I'm quite focused. Truth be known, with just 5 km remaining now, and a little over 20 minutes before I can retire from marathon running for ever, I am without doubt more focused than at any point in any previous race.

A dull pain has gradually come on in my legs. I'm working hard. I'm having to dig deep. I need to concentrate. I can't possibly blow it at this stage. I've come too far to fail now. I grit my teeth, push on through the pain and try to focus on my posture. I mustn't slouch. I remain as upright and as tall as I can, but it's not easy.

There's one key factor that I'm confident is going to make the difference - well, two factors if the beetroot juice does its thing. I incorporated a new session into my training this time around, thanks to my attendance at a seminar hosted by Richard. (That'll be '2 hours 8 minutes' Richard!) I shared the room with a group of elite athletes for whom the concept of being unable to break 3 hours must be incomprehensible. Whilst I felt somewhat out of place in such company, the key message of the seminar was as applicable to me as it was to Dan Robinson, not only the fastest marathoner in the room, but presently the fastest marathoner in Britain!

The topic of the seminar was the importance of the long tempo run in any marathon training schedule. Not to be confused with the usual long Sunday run, the long tempo run is to be considered a tough quality session, necessitating not much more than a relatively easy run the day preceding it, and an equally gentle recovery run the day following. The distance to be covered in the session should gradually be increased over the weeks from around 13 miles to 20 miles, with the first half being a tad slower than marathon pace, the second half being a smidgeon faster, with the final tenth of the overall distance being flat out. The purpose of the session is to get the body used to working hard when tired, and become accustomed to adopting the most efficient strategy for an elite marathon time, that is a race of 'negative splits', meaning covering the second half in slightly less time than the first.

For me, the specific learning point which I took away from Richard's seminar was that if I am to feel strong beyond 20 miles and through the latter stages of the marathon, a regular churning-out of the long tempo run is to be an essential piece in the marathon training jigsaw.

The message was supported by evidence of an array of high profile marathon winning times linked to the inclusion of such sessions in these athletes' training schedules. Of particular interest was the fact that it is only since the turn of the century that the Kenyans and Ethiopians have regularly been winning the major world marathons, and it is only in these recent years that they have incorporated the long tempo run as a core session in their programmes. The London Marathon, for example, has been won by a Kenyan or Ethiopian every year from 2003 to 2011. In the previous two decades, excepting a Kenyan victory in 1989, the heroes of London were a broad spread of nationalities from US, Norway, UK, Japan, Denmark, Russia, Portugal, Mexico, Spain and Morocco.

As part of the seminar, Richard had arranged for Allison (previously an international runner, now fully fledged coach) to interview Dan. As she sought to draw out inspiring words of wisdom from Britain's best, what unfolded in front of us all was a rather surprising laid-back personality, clearly an utter natural at his game, unknowingly delivering ripples of envy through his audience.

Having received a raft of tips from Allison, I have come to realise that she is a strong believer in the inclusion of drills, stretching, strength work, massage and the like. However, as we all looked to the man on stage for an insight into his secrets, it became apparent that these were not regular features of his training regime. Also, contrary to the norm for most top marathoners, most of his long runs were carried out on a treadmill, and on race day there didn't seem to be any structured in-taking of fuel. Knowing Allison as I do, I could sense her desire to take Dan under her wing and knock a good couple of minutes off his marathon PB.

The following morning, I did not personally take part in the pre-arranged 20 km tempo run as I had only recently set about another of my multitude of comebacks from some injury or other. I offered my services as 'lead bike' to hopefully prevent the athletes from getting lost cruising up and down Brighton's sea front promenade. There was a staggered start dictated by one's current marathon time. The session incorporated an 'out and back' course, turning at the 5 km point, returning to the start to make 10 km, then repeating that 10 km ideally a bit faster. Structuring the route as such meant that any wind should not distort the times for each half of the session.

For a post-run breakfast and comparing of split times, we returned to the hotel where the seminar had taken place. The event had been a success - everyone had achieved negative splits!

I was sitting a few places from Dan at the breakfast table, wondering if some healthy 'super-food' meal might unlock the secret of his success... but no, the preferred post-run snack was a full fry-up. I concluded that if Dan and I could combine his natural talent with my attention to detail, we would surely witness the first ever sub 2 hour marathon.

Having taken on board the importance of the long tempo run, I have knocked out a fair number of them in the past few months, each time struggling with the addition of an extra mile or two, but finishing hard, caning the last stretch! It is right now that the hard work is put to the test. I am clearly benefiting as this is the first time that I have ever gone through mile 23 still inside 3 hour pace. I lost a few seconds between miles 22 and 23. I can accommodate that, but I can't afford to slow any more.

My breathing becomes more laboured. I anxiously rip the last gel from my wrist band and tear it open to force the contents into my system, giving myself a final kick of caffeine. Everything's hurting. My calves haven't seized up, but they're heavy, and so are my quads. I'm hungry. I'm feeling weak, but I can't think about that.

I look at my Garmin more frequently now to see that I'm holding on. I'm maintaining pace. No, damn it, I'm not maintaining pace. This is where the Garmin is not accurate enough to be of any value as the displayed pacing keeps jumping around. It seems an absolute eternity before I go through mile 25.

I'm dropping off the pace badly. My left hip's tightening, one of the consequences of my left leg being 1.5 cm longer than the right. This is despite wearing orthotics to combat the imbalance. I was aware of the discomfort a mile or so ago. It wasn't bothering me earlier, but it is now.

I have another gear though. I always have another gear. That's one of my strengths - no matter how hard the last mile I've always got a fast finish.

I try to work out how long I took for the previous mile but I'm too tired to think straight. For the past 25 miles, my mind has been occupied by calculations as if in an all-morning maths exam. Since 9 o'clock, I've been constantly assessing the time taken so as to fathom out what pace I need to average for the remainder of the course, such that I can be done by mid-day. With every second gained and lost, the emotional rollercoaster has worn me down.

I briefly consult my pacing bracelet. I know I'm running at slower than 6:52 per mile now, which is what I'd need for an even-paced 3 hour marathon. I built up a small margin earlier on, but I think the weaving and the water station congestion have cost me dearly.

I give it everything I've got but I'm tiring. I've run a mile in just under five minutes on the track. Surely I can find enough energy for a final kick to get me through the last mile in about 6 minutes 30 seconds. I dig deep. All I need to do is run a 6:30 mile! It can't be that difficult, I've done it hundreds of times. Come on! I simply cannot fail. I'm well on course for a PB but that's not good enough. A PB is not what I'm here for. This last mile is beginning to feel like a full marathon in its own right. I don't remember anyone fixing lead weights to my ankles but that's just what it feels like.

The Brandenburg Gate comes into view. I stop looking at my watch.

My legs are turning to jelly but I give it my all. I stride out as fast as I possibly can through the Gate and, with about 400m to go, I find myself overtaking other runners. No-one's coming past me. I'm the one who's doing the overtaking. With no more than 200m to go, a runner collapses in front of me. I swerve around him. I look up at the clock above the finish line. It has already passed 3 hours, but I pay no attention to it. It's not a reflection of my own personal time as I took 18 seconds to cross the start line after the gun was fired.

I know I've not made it though. Despite all the carbo-loading over the last few days and the gels consumed throughout the past 26.2 miles, I have felt my energy dwindling away in the latter stages. Mental strength has been defeated by pain and fatigue. There might have been a slight kick over the last 400m but, with legs of jelly and nothing left in the tank, once again this is not to be my day. I have finished in 3:00:42.

Chapter 9

Lawnmower, Broom and Bag of Compost

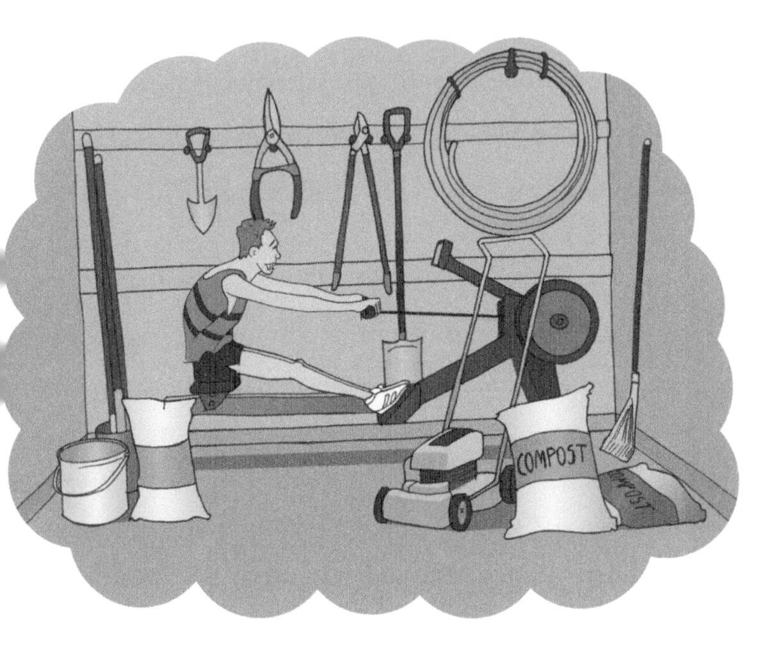

Despite Berlin not allowing me a sub-3, I didn't beat myself up over it.

I think, for the first time in eight marathons, I came away focusing on the positives - and in fact there were several reasons to be pleased. Of great importance, I had beaten Neil. But apart from that, I ran a PB. Not just a little PB, I had knocked 78 seconds off my previous best, and was six minutes faster than my debut marathon completed when I was 15 years younger. I've defied the ageing process!

I could see the funny side of yet another miss even as I was a few yards from crossing the finish line. And the hours which followed, having a celebratory beer with my mates in the Berlin sunshine, made me realise the real reason I keep doing this. It's because it's done in fabulous company.

I have a wonderful group of friends whom I have come to know through running over the past 15 years. There was the usual mix of outcomes that day. Some dropped out, others didn't even make it to the start line, some narrowly missed a PB. And then there was Fiona. Having previously fainted in London at mile 20, in Berlin she smashed her PB, knocking seven minutes off her previous best to finish in 2:46, making her the fifth British female. It almost didn't matter who did what that day. We were all in it together, proud and overjoyed for those who had achieved, but sharing the disappointment of those who had to pull out with injury. We had spent months training together, taking it in turns to get ill and injured, and it would have been extremely unlikely for all of us to have met expectations in one race.

Our weekend in Berlin had been a success.

The following day, back at home, I took a closer look at my Garmin. It seemed to take great delight in pointing out that I had in fact run three tenths of a mile too far, which of course would go a fair way to justifying my taking 43 seconds too long. According to the Garmin, I had covered 26.5 miles, as opposed to the correct marathon distance of 26.2.

This made perfect sense. 26.2 miles was represented by a painted blue line in the road, which followed the inside bends and indicated the shortest route around the course. The leaders in the race, having heaps of space around them, would have pretty much stuck to the painted line for the entire route. I, on the other hand, couldn't get close to it, adding a few metres to my marathon at every bend. Combined with my erratic veering left and right to fight to get to the water stations, I could totally see how I might have run an extra 0.3 of a mile - put another way, approximately 1% over-distance. So, if I took 3:00:42 to cover 26.5 miles, by interpolation that means I took 2:58:40 to do 26.2.

That means ... I couldn't believe it ... Yes! Yes!! Yes!!! ... I've run a marathon in under 3 hours!

But I haven't, have I.

It doesn't count! My official time is 3:00:42 and there will always be a question mark over whether the 0.3 over-distance was down to Garmin error. More than ever though now, I know I can break 3 hours. I've done it ... unofficially!

It normally takes me about a month before I can run again after a marathon, with battered legs first having to learn to walk again. Bizarrely, post Berlin, I was back jogging around the streets of Brighton after just a couple of days. I can only put this down to the fact that I had done most of my Berlin training on a flat road, which meant I had got my legs used to the repetitive pounding. Having trained mostly off-road for my previous marathons, the subsequent shock of 26.2 miles on the road had wrecked me.

Mark persuaded me to go for a 10k PB in Dartford just three weeks after Berlin.

I was reluctant to do so, preferring to give my body a little longer to recover. I deferred making a decision to run Dartford until the day before the race. However, Mark convinced me that I should make the most of all the training I had done in the preceding months, so I took his advice and joined him for the hour drive there on the Sunday morning.

I set off hard and maintained fourth position the whole way round. I smashed my 36:42 PB of 10 years earlier, finishing in 36:16.

A week later, on my 102nd Hove parkrun, I got a 5k PB of 17:34.

Two weeks later, I ran the Barns Green Half Marathon in 1:23:41 (my best half marathon for ten years) and after a further fortnight I secured a course best in my 10th running of the Brighton 10k.

It had been a great month - three PBs in four weeks! My narrowly missing sub-3 in Berlin paled into insignificance.

For the first time in 15 years, I then decided to completely refrain from running for three weeks.

I had previously taken long blocks of time out on numerous occasions, but always enforced due to illness or injury. On this occasion, though, having trained hard for five months and raced hard for two, I took it upon myself to give my body a well-earned rest.

After my rest, I eased myself slowly back into running with just a few short jogs here and there, but I needed a new focus. Well... that wasn't difficult... I had unfinished business.

I had never attempted two marathons in any one year. After Berlin, though, I had recovered well. I had continued to race well, I had given my body a good rest, and I had remained injury-free. It was an easy decision to enter the 2012 Brighton Marathon the following April.

One slight problem - entries were closed. I didn't think to enter earlier as Berlin was supposed to be my last ever marathon. I dropped Richard (as in '2 hours 8 minutes' Richard / mate of Haile Gebrselassie) an email. He's involved with the organisation of the Brighton Marathon. I hoped that if I were to grovel politely, he'd get me a place.

It was my lucky day. He had a handful of reserve places left. I was in!

Having planned a three-week holiday in Australia over the Christmas and New Year I figured that, with some base training in place during the preceding few weeks, I would commence proper training as soon as I arrived Down Under. I spent my first week striding up and down the Great Ocean Road on Australia's south coast... 56 miles of it to be precise.

It was hilly. I wasn't used to hills.

I strained my left Achilles tendon. I eased back a bit the following week.

I wanted to give the Melbourne parkrun my best shot. So, on the Saturday morning, with rested legs and following a night out on the beer, off I headed to Albert Park.

Somehow, I came first! Of all the tens of thousands of people who have completed a parkrun somewhere in the world, I would be surprised if there is anyone other than myself who, embarrassingly, has the slowest recorded win on two separate continents. To date, there have been 153 Hove parkruns and I am the only person to have won one in a time slower than 20 minutes. I won the eighth Albert Park parkrun in 18:49. No one else has won on this course in slower than 18:27. But who cares?! A win's a win! You have to be in it to win it! (Ooh, apologies again, Mr Sinton-Hewitt, I haven't won at all, have I!?)

And so the process begins all over again...

Well, it doesn't quite have to begin all over again - only six-and-a-half months will have lapsed between Berlin and Brighton.

I have taken the view that by doing a second marathon inside a year, my Berlin training and associated races will serve as a good platform on which to build. Once again, I take on board Albert Einstein's definition of insanity ("Doing the same thing over and over again and expecting different results"). I have decided to increase my weekly mileage... and run my tempo runs at a faster pace. This way, I shall get used to running my long runs faster, with a view to quickening my pace on race day.

I think it would also make sense to practise grabbing drinks whilst running. As far as I'm aware, it'll be plastic bottles in Brighton, not cups! There will be fewer drink stations than in Berlin, but I shall be more than happy to reimburse, in pints of beer or otherwise, an appropriate number of non-running friends for situating themselves strategically along the course to hand me suitable refreshments.

I shall also factor in some hill reps in preparation for the incline on St James's Street.

As regards the matter of fuelling, I have identified a couple of ways in which I believe I can improve my race-day performance.

In the past, I have always been a big eater and, after all, everyone seems to bang on about the importance of piling on the carbs. However, I have decided to skip breakfast - at least, to not have breakfast until back from my morning run. Apparently, by getting the body used to burning fat (an inherently inefficient process), rather than relying on recently-consumed glycogen, one better prepares oneself for the marathon's latter stages when all glycogen stores are depleted. In an ideal world my pre-race carbo-loading, along with appropriate ingestion of glycogen en route, would fend off the need to dip into body-fat stores. However, if I do become depleted of glycogen, which I have at the tail end of every marathon I've ever run, at least I shall hopefully have trained my body to put my minimal body fat to use in as efficient a manner as possible.

I also wonder if I have, in the past, relied too much on energy gels during my long training runs. I figure that, by staying away from them in training, maybe I shall get my body used to consuming nothing but water and so not become reliant on the gels. My thinking is that they'll then have a more positive impact on the big day.

This has to work! All I need to find is 43 seconds. I'm not getting any younger and I'm running out of things to try.

Up until late January, training went according to plan.

I adhered to Pfitzinger and Douglas's training programme, which I had followed in preparation for Berlin, but banged out greater weekly mileage. My confidence level was greater than for any of my previous eight marathons. I had completed a fair number of runs at much faster than 3 hour marathon pace, such that I felt I could easily churn out the 26.2 miles well inside the required 6:52 per mile.

Unfortunately, by early February it was a case of *déjà vu*.

I was too ambitious. I had stepped up my weekly mileage too dramatically and wrecked my left Achilles. It seems I had torn the sheath that surrounds the tendon to such an extent that even slow walking was painful. There was no way I could run even a few steps.

This was a major blow.

So much for building on my successes of Berlin and subsequent races to go for a sub-3 in Brighton in the April! It was not going to get the better of me, though.

I decided to maintain my fitness by cross-training. Running was painful, as was cycling, but I discovered that I could row and swim without any problem. Almost every day for five weeks, I rowed and swam. I had converted my garage into a small gym, which included an old rowing machine purchased secondhand from Steve for a crate of beer. Not exclusively a gym, the garage was also a store room for gardening equipment. Like a man possessed, I repeatedly found myself oscillating my body to and fro, staring at lawnmower, broom and bag of compost.

Having gradually increased both the duration and pace of these sessions, by the end of five weeks, I was knocking out sessions like 15 x 5 minutes, yet I had no idea whether this remotely correlated with the running I ought to have been doing. But I was determined to maintain fitness and give myself the best possible chance of bringing my marathon career to a successful close, so crammed in as much swimming and rowing as my body would allow before and after work each day. I also regularly followed

Ryan Giggs's fitness DVD - a 90-minute routine of stretching and strength exercises. I figured that if it allowed one of the oldest football players in the English Premiership to continue to be selected to play for one of the best teams in the world, it was good enough for me!

I returned to running on 7th March, just five weeks and four days before the Brighton Marathon. Mindful of the need to ease back into running gradually and also allowing for a 10-day taper, this left only three weeks for any kind of quality training.

My first jog back was a struggle and it became immediately apparent that I had run out of time. I may have maintained a reasonable level of fitness, but I was well out of practice in terms of actual running.

I consulted Nick again (as in Nick, the top-notch doctor / physiotherapist / god I have kept in business for the last 15 years). He strongly advised me not to run Brighton. This came as no surprise. I knew full well that I was going to have to ditch any prospect of a sub-3 in Brighton, and instead find an alternative marathon later in the year. In fact, come race day in Brighton as I cycled at a leisurely pace up and down the sea front, supporting various friends whose Achilles tendons were in full working order, my left one continued to give me jip. Conceding defeat and deferring marathon retirement was definitely the correct decision.

It was time for Nick to set to work with another needle. There was a fifty-fifty chance that a cortisone injection would do the trick. If it didn't fix me, the only alternative would be for me to wear an enormous boot designed to restrict movement in my left ankle until the tear had fully healed. This could take a couple of weeks or more.

With summer approaching, I couldn't envisage any of my shorts being complemented by the wearing of a humongous boot on my left foot. It wasn't a look I relished and I desperately hoped that Nick had stabbed my ankle in the right spot. He had! I carefully adhered to his instructions to take things really easy over the following seven days and the injection proved to be a success. All pain had gone for good.

I set about my research to select the marathon most likely to allow me to finish what I'd started one-and-a-half decades ago. With age using everything in its armoury to stand in my tracks, it wasn't just the training I needed to get right. In order to maximise my chances of success, first I had to find a marathon which would meet various criteria.

The timing of the event was crucial.

I had followed Pfitzinger and Douglas's 18-week training schedule for Berlin, albeit with the start of the 18 weeks immediately following a come-back from injury. That meant the first two to three weeks were taken up with a gradual re-introduction to running, the consequence being that my proper marathon training was effectively reduced to 15 weeks. Now, in preparation for my final marathon, I figured I should allow not only a full 18 weeks for quality training, but also an initial recovery period of eight weeks. In doing so, I would be giving myself plenty of time for my Achilles to thoroughly heal and re-gain strength, and also develop a base level of fitness, ready to attack the 18-week schedule with 100% commitment.

With regard to the topography of my chosen course, it goes without saying that I would need a flat road. This whittled down my options significantly, particularly when taking into account the avoidance of cobbles, as well as my preference for smooth tarmac.

Being blessed with perfect weather would be impossible to guarantee, but at least I could go for a location where the conditions were most likely to be in my favour. I needed a cold day, but not freezing, and no wind. If it was going to rain, a light drizzle or damp atmosphere would be good, but I'd prefer to avoid a heavy downpour. Not only do damp clothes restrict movement, the accumulated water also brings about unnecessary weight gain!

So, I needed a flat course on a cold day around late October. Preferring to exclude any marathon involving a long haul flight and an extensive time difference, there was one obvious choice... Amsterdam, 21st October.

Chapter 10

Guinness or Murphy's??

David the Architect had also previously mentioned that he fancied Amsterdam.

I had met David the Architect through Hove parkrun and he had also come on the Berlin trip, although I hadn't known him so well back then. I tried to drum up a few other mates to make it into a group trip. However, most of my marathon-running mates had already done London or Brighton in the spring and didn't fancy another in the autumn. I did manage, though, to persuade a few to enter the Amsterdam Half Marathon taking place on the same day. So, we had a group! And I looked forward to the social aspect of our trip across the Channel to the land of the windmill.

Unfortunately, owing to a distinct lack of anyone else preparing for an autumn marathon, except for David the Architect who was targeting a sub-3:30 PB, Norman No Mates was faced with the mentally challenging prospect of four months of hard training on his Jack Jones. This indeed proved to be mentally challenging!

For the first few jogs at the start of my eight-week torn-Achilles-recovery phase, I could think of no-one slow enough to accompany me. My debut post-cortisone run was a single pathetic mile, broken into three sections with a couple of two-minute recovery walks. The total running time for the mile was 10 minutes 30 seconds. The most unfit person I knew could probably have walked faster with a bag of cement on each shoulder.

It didn't take much analysis to conclude what I had to do. Basically, I had almost six months to be able to run my mile without the two-minute interludes, knock at least 3 minutes 38 seconds off (for the required 6:52-per-mile pace) and then do that continuously, 26.2 times.

During the first three weeks, I ran just every other day, each time either increasing the distance by a small increment or running at a slightly faster pace. This was boring, but necessary. By the end of the eight-week torn-Achilles-recovery phase, I was up to 47 miles per week, with my longest run being 14.5 miles and averaging 7:54-per-mile. This was still too slow by 1 minute 2 seconds per mile and only just over half the race distance covered, but that was fine. I was totally over the injury and was able to get stuck in to my marathon programme with a two-month base behind me.

I make a comprehensive list of all the factors, to be taken into account, which will contribute to marginal gains in my performance. Making a list is not wholly necessary as such factors have become deeply ingrained over many years, a few new ones added to the list with each under-performance.

One key factor stands out above all the others... remain injury-free! Over the years, I have been forced into taking time out on far too many occasions to mention. And without doubt, when I have enjoyed long, unbroken periods of consistent training, my best performances have followed. I figure that if I can get through 18 weeks of training without disaster, not only would that be a first, I believe it would also have the most significant influence on a successful outcome in Amsterdam.

I think about the times I've got injured. They have typically been a result of pushing too hard, deciding mid-session to speed up, maybe try and race someone faster than me when I should have been doing a steady-pace run. I have to admit there have been times when I have set out on a recovery jog along Brighton's seafront promenade, subsequently switching, mid-run, into competitive mode when overtaken by someone I think really shouldn't be coming past me.

I now visualise such moments and remind myself, time and time again, of the importance of remaining injury-free. This is a marathon, not a sprint!

The weeks pass by and I find myself averaging about 60 miles per week. The first couple of months entail very little speed work, being more about building an endurance base. Occasionally I'm joined on a training run by Neil, Shaun and Goat Boy, although rarely for my whole run.

They have no reason to run as far as me - they're not training for a marathon!

My social life has diminished into the odd evening out, maybe once a week, but always home in time for an early night in preparation for whatever session Pfitzinger and Douglas have lined up for me the following day - as well as a day at work. And I regularly decline offers from friends to meet up at the beach after work for an ice cream or a barbecue. I have training to do! I even turn down a surfing weekend in Devon, with two months to go, taking the view that a drive of several hours each way will eat into valuable training time. And I wouldn't want to risk the possibility of falling off a wave and causing myself an injury.

Summer rapidly descends into autumn and, with it, long, dark evenings. I can no longer train on the Downs. I know I did the majority of my training for Berlin on the road but, with the increased volume of training for Amsterdam, I have been persuaded by many experienced marathoners to carry out the bulk of my longer runs off-road so as to reduce the chances of injury. Whenever possible, I carry out my work from home to avoid a commute. This enables me to jump straight into my running kit at 5:30pm, maximising whatever daylight remains and at least do part of my run off-road.

I'm finding it harder and harder to stand up to the boredom of this all-consuming mission. I desperately want to turn the clocks forward to the moment I enter Amsterdam's Olympic Stadium at the end of the marathon, with a couple of minutes to spare to comfortably finish inside 3 hours.

By mid-September, the training shoes I've been wearing almost every day for the last two months have worn out. Ordinarily, this wouldn't present a problem. I don't let my shoes get so worn out that they are beyond use. However, as I pop in to see Sam at the Jog Shop to replace them with a couple of pairs of the same, I discover that the model I have become used to over the last 15 months is now obsolete.

I try the new model that supersedes mine. They don't fit! I curse the shoe manufacturer.

This is not the first time I have tried to replace a pair of worn out shoes to find the model that fitted me perfectly well has been ditched for a newer version, slightly different in some way, making it totally unfit for my purpose.

I try other local running shops. None of them any longer stock my favourites.

By the time I eventually get around to tracking down a pair on the internet, I have clocked up another 100 miles or so in my now totally trashed pair. Surprise surprise – I develop a pain on the underside of both feet. I continue to curse the shoe manufacturer. I decide to wipe out the stock of the online supplier, relieving them of their last seven pairs. Hopefully this will defer the problem for another couple of years and, more importantly, see me through the balance of my marathon training.

In the meantime, although I have taken delivery of the new footwear, they need to be broken in. This, of course, means I can't yet use them for my longer runs which, of course, means I have no choice but to continue wearing the old knackered ones.

My feet hurt!

There are eight weeks remaining before my assault on Amsterdam. I decide to book in to see Nick for an ultrasound scan on my feet as I fear I may be developing plantar fasciitis. Every runner I know who has had the misfortune of suffering this over-use injury has been forced to rest for several months. A dark shadow is cast over my hopes for a sub-3 any time soon, as every training session is painful.

Fortunately the scan confirms no plantar fasciitis – more of a tendon issue.

The remaining few weeks of training continues to be uncomfortable. I continue to curse the shoe manufacturer.

I find, though, that I can manage the problem by regular icing, massage and application of anti-inflammatory gel. I am determined that this is not going to get the better of me. I have thrown so much time and money at this ridiculous goal, I absolutely cannot give up. Flights and accommodation are booked. I am going to Amsterdam to break 3 hours, no matter how much work is required and no matter how much discomfort needs to be suffered to get there.

I have come to realise over the years that, in order to achieve the best possible result, it is an absolute necessity for profound discomfort to be suffered in both the training and the actual race.

And in training for Amsterdam I have, more than ever, applied the principle that race pain is indirectly proportionate to training pain. If the hard training runs are executed half-heartedly, there's an almost certainty that the marathon, particularly in the latter stages, will be a most unpleasant experience. On the other hand, in order to enjoy a vaguely comfortable ride on race day, a combination of grit, determination, tiredness, forever-aching muscles, mental toughness, deep soul searching, and compromise in social life (I could go on) must all feature throughout the months of preparation.

I enter a couple of short races in the lead-up to Amsterdam, so as to put my training to the test.

Firstly, the Birthday Boys 5000m track race in Withdean Stadium – an annual event to mark the birthdays of several of my running mates, all within a few days of each other.

Undecided as to whether to run my marathon in trainers or racing shoes, I decide to put my racers to the test at the Birthday Boys race. Although only a low-key occasion, I am delighted to knock out a 17:21 PB. I subsequently study a conversion table, which informs me I am on course for a 2:49 marathon. I absorb this information with caution, owing to the fact that virtually every race I have ever run would suggest I should crack 3 hours. Nonetheless, this is a great confidence booster.

The following day, I'm on a flight to Ireland for the Dingle Half Marathon.

From the moment I entered this a few months ago, Dingle was only ever meant to be a jolly, a weekend on the black stuff, incorporating a 13.1 mile fun run. Part of the reason for my deciding not to hammer it is because the course is a hilly tarmac road, on which I don't imagine I'll be doing my legs any favours by striding out hard on the downhill sections.

I again deliberate over a decision on trainers or racers. I decide on racers on the grounds that the outcome will steer me towards the most appropriate footwear to take to Holland.

My only dilemma now on the eve of the Dingle Half is do I drink Guinness or Murphy's?

I don't ponder over this for too long. I go for both! I'm accompanied by Glasses Chris who will also be running the Half tomorrow and Mark who has favoured the 50-miler option. Mark's race begins at the crack of dawn, so is time-restricted to only managing four pints before he and his support crew retire for the evening. Glasses Chris and I sample one more pub for a fifth pint and then head back to our hotel. I hit the sack at around 1am.

The following morning's breakfast and a strong coffee help to sort out my hangover, although I still feel a little jaded as I start warming up. But miraculously, as I commence my habitual three reps of 80m accelerations just five minutes before the start, I begin to come back to life.

The road is indeed rather hilly, a point-to-point course with the finish some 40m higher than the start, and a fair bit into strong wind.

I repeatedly glance at my Garmin and am most surprised by my pace. Behind me, 1800 runners; in front, just a handful!

By half way, I'm on course to beat my half-marathon PB which was set 14 years ago. This is no longer a fun run, it' a race!

I am totally amazed to come 6th out of 1757 finishers anc just two places behind Chris's 4th. I've finished in 1:22:41 missing my PB by 5 seconds, although I figure it's worth PB on account of the hills and the wind. It soon transpire that I was first in the 'over 40' age group. I am presentec with a spread of prizes. This is better than Christmas - hat tee shirt, sweatshirt, free entry for next year, glass trophy embarrassingly large bottle of champagne and a chequ for 150 Euros. (Not bad for a B-team jogger!)

This gives me another huge boost in confidence. Surely, i I remain injury-free for the next seven weeks and continu to stick to my training plan, I will definitely be able tc bring my mission to a close on 21st October. I am alsc reassured by the fact that this time last year, seven week before Berlin, I only managed 1:26:08 for the South Coas Half Marathon - and that was a flat course!

With three weeks to go, I reduce my weekly mileag slightly, focusing more on speed work than endurance.

With two weeks to go, I knock out a 10 km time trial ir Hove Park, which I complete in 36:56. I am not at all fazec by this being 40 seconds outside of my PB. On th contrary, I am encouraged by my performance on th park's undulating circuit, with gusting wind and withou company, at the end of what has been a hard training week. And I've run it 1 minute 10 seconds faster than the 10 km time trial I did on Brighton's flat seafront promenade last year, two weeks prior to Berlin.

The undersides of my feet are still sore. There has been no set-up in the last five weeks but, with regular icing and massage, the pain has not worsened.

10 days remain. The training is done. My focus is now on tapering my mileage, lots of rest between sessions, doing everything in my control to avoid catching a cold, and more frequent visits to Kader (the brutal massage therapist).

I learn from the official Amsterdam Marathon website that the sports drink being provided is AA-Drink Iso-Lemon. Never heard of it! I email them to find out where I can purchase some so as to experiment with it and ensure that it and my stomach are compatible. No joy! You can't buy it! Never mind, I track down a comment on a blog, which suggests that it's not too dissimilar to other isotonic drinks I've tried and got on with.

However, I am more than perturbed to learn that it's going to be served in cups. This is disastrous news. Berlin all over again! I immediately reach in my kitchen cupboard for a paper cup left over from a barbecue. I repeatedly half-fill it with water and practise grabbing it from different angles, applying varying degrees of force to squeeze the top, thereby narrowing the opening with a view to minimising spillage.

My shirt is now drenched.

I have built up quite a thirst with all the stress and over-exertion, so I pour myself a glass of water and decide to get in a bit more practice later on.

I have already concluded, post-Dingle, that I shall be wearing racing shoes. However, as they are a tad battered from having carried my weight through a number of races, there will clearly be an advantage to be gained by replacing them with new ones of the same. A wave of panic ensues as I discover that the shoe manufacturer has brought out a revised model. They don't fit! They're narrower than mine and no running store in Brighton has any of mine left in stock. I curse the shoe manufacturer! Again!

My sole mission in life right now is to track down a pair online. Every other aspect of my life is temporarily on hold. My online running-shoe supplier again comes to the rescue. I pay whatever is necessary to guarantee delivery the next day.

There is just one week remaining.